WHAT EVERY PRINCIPAL SHOULD KNOW ABOUT

SCHOOL-COMMUNITY LEADERSHIP

WHAT EVERY PRINCIPAL SHOULD KNOW ABOUT LEADERSHIP
The 7-Book Collection

By Jeffrey Glanz

What Every Principal Should Know About Instructional Leadership

What Every Principal Should Know About Cultural Leadership

What Every Principal Should Know About Ethical and Spiritual Leadership

What Every Principal Should Know About School-Community Leadership

What Every Principal Should Know About Collaborative Leadership

What Every Principal Should Know About Operational Leadership

What Every Principal Should Know About Strategic Leadership

WHAT EVERY PRINCIPAL SHOULD KNOW ABOUT

SCHOOL-COMMUNITY LEADERSHIP

JEFFREY GLANZ

CORWIN PRESS
A SAGE Publications Company
Thousand Oaks, California

For information:

Corwin Press
A Sage Publications Company
2455 Teller Road
Thousand Oaks, California 91320
E-mail: order@corwinpress.com

Sage Publications Ltd.
1 Oliver's Yard
55 City Road
London EC1Y 1SP
United Kingdom

Sage Publications India Pvt. Ltd.
B-42, Panchsheel Enclave
Post Box 4109
New Delhi 110 017 India

Printed in the United States of America.

Library of Congress Cataloging-in-Publication Data

Glanz, Jeffrey.
What every principal should know about school-community leadership / Jeffrey Glanz.
        p. cm.
Includes bibliographical references and index.
ISBN 1-4129-1589-9 (pbk.)
    1. Community and school—United States. 2. School principals—United States.
3. Educational leadership—United States. 4. School improvement programs—
United States. I. Title.
LC221.G53 2006
371.19—dc22   2005015849
This book is printed on acid-free paper.

05   06   07   08   09   10   9   8   7   6   5   4   3   2   1

Acquisitions Editor:	Elizabeth Brenkus
Editorial Assistant:	Candice L. Ling
Project Editor:	Tracy Alpern
Copy Editor:	Colleen Brennan
Proofreader:	Christine Dahlin
Typesetter:	C&M Digitals (P) Ltd.
Indexer:	Gloria Tierney
Cover Designer:	Rose Storey
Graphic Designer:	Scott Van Atta

Contents

*To Scott Miller, Vincenza Gallassio,
Karina Constantino, Joseph Martucci,
and other school colleagues who inspire me
with their commitment to high-quality education
for all and who remain steadfast in their belief in strong
school-community relations. Any deficiencies in this work
should not be attributed to them; they are educational exemplars.*

Acknowledgments

I once worked with a principal who, it seemed to me at the time, placed an inordinate amount of effort in working with members of the community external to the school building itself. "Don't you think," I naively said to him, "we should be spending *all* our time focusing on student learning *in* the building?" With a reserve sense of calm, patience, and mentorship, he responded, "Jeffrey, you're right. We must continue to focus our work with one end in mind and that is helping each boy and girl in this school succeed academically and otherwise. But," and this is when he made me aware that our work in school does not occur in isolation from other forces and activities external to the school, "we can't go it alone. . . . If we are able to build strong coalitions with key members of the community that can, for instance, provide us with financial and other resources that help build educational programs in the school, then we will be indeed focusing all our efforts at helping our children learn and, most importantly, succeed in life." Good principals know this to be true. They work arduously to build and sustain school-community partnerships because they know that such partnerships can make the difference. This book, and series, is dedicated to all who aspire to the principalship, currently serve as a principal, or who have been a principal and who believe in such work. No nobler an enterprise and profession exists, for principals are the ones who spend a good portion of their time in forging meaningful school-community partnerships that might not otherwise bring much-needed resources (personnel and material) into the school building in order to promote and sustain academic excellence for all students.

* * * * * * * * * * * * * * * *

Thanks to Mrs. Liz DeForest, a parent coordinator in a New York City school, who provided insights into this newly created position. Thanks to Mr. Lester Kostick for sharing ideas he used as principal to foster school-community relations. Vincenza Gallassio, a principal in Staten Island, New York, shared her expertise as well. Thanks to acquisitions editor Lizzie Brenkus for her gentle encouragement, support, and willingness to help me think things through. Her keen guidance helped me frame the contents of this book to contrast another book in this series on collaborative leadership. Much thanks also goes to Robb Clouse, editorial director, who prompted me to consider a trilogy of sorts: a book about teaching, which eventuated into *Teaching 101*; a book about assistant principals, which led to *The Assistant Principal's Handbook*; and a book about principals, which resulted, to my surprise, in this groundbreaking series, *What Every Principal Should Know About Leadership*.

Special thanks to my wife, Lisa, without whose support such a venture would be impossible. I love you . . . at least as much as I love writing.

Corwin Press gratefully acknowledges the contributions of the following individuals:

Regina Birdsell, Principal
Academy School
Madison, CT

Jeff C. Jones, Executive
Assistant to the Chief
  Superintendent
Calgary Board
  of Education
Calgary, AB

Glenn Sewell, Principal/
  Superintendent
Wheatland Union High
  School District
Wheatland, CA

Paul Young, Author/
  Executive Director
West After School Center
Lancaster, OH

About the Author

 **Jeffrey Glanz, EdD**, currently serves as Dean of Graduate Programs and Chair of the Department of Education at Wagner College in Staten Island, New York. He also coordinates the educational leadership program that leads to New York State certification as a principal or assistant principal. Prior to arriving at Wagner, he served as executive assistant to the president of Kean University in Union, New Jersey. Dr. Glanz held faculty status as a tenured professor in the Department of Instruction and Educational Leadership at Kean University's College of Education. He was named Graduate Teacher of the Year in 1999 by the Student Graduate Association and was also that year's recipient of the Presidential Award for Outstanding Scholarship. He served as an administrator and teacher in the New York City public schools for 20 years. Dr. Glanz has authored, coauthored, or coedited 13 books and has more than 35 peer-reviewed article publications. With Corwin Press he coauthored the bestselling *Supervision That Improves Teaching* (2nd ed.) and *Supervision in Practice: Three Steps to Improve Teaching and Learning* and authored *The Assistant Principal's Handbook* and *Teaching 101: Strategies for the Beginning Teacher.* More recently, he coauthored *Building Effective Learning Communities: Strategies for Leadership, Learning, & Collaboration.* Most recently, Dr. Glanz has authored the *What Every Principal Should Know About Leadership: The 7-Book Collection:*

What Every Principal Should Know About Instructional Leadership

What Every Principal Should Know About Cultural Leadership

What Every Principal Should Know About Ethical and Spiritual Leadership

What Every Principal Should Know About School-Community Leadership

What Every Principal Should Know About Collaborative Leadership

What Every Principal Should Know About Operational Leadership

What Every Principal Should Know About Strategic Leadership

Consult his Web site for additional information: http://www .wagner.edu/faculty/users/jglanz/web/.

* * * * * * * * * * * * * * * *

The "About the Author" information you've just glanced at (excuse the pun . . . my name? . . . Glanz, "glance"?!) is standard author bio info you find in most books. As you'll discover if you glance at . . . I mean *read* . . . the Introduction, I want this book to be user-friendly in several ways. One of the ways is that I want to write as I would converse with you in person. Therefore, I prefer in most places to use the first person, so please excuse the informality. Although we've likely never met, we really do know each other if you think about it. We share a common passion about leadership, school building leadership to be more precise. We share many similar experiences. In an experiential, almost spiritual, sense, we have much in common. What I write about directly relates, I hope, to your lived experience. The information in this volume, as with the entire series, is meant to resonate, stir, provoke, and provide ideas about principal leadership, which is vital in order to promote excellence and achievement for all.

This traditional section of a book is titled "About the Author." The first paragraph in this section tells you what I "do," not "about" me or who I am. I won't bore you with all details "about me," but I'd like just to share one bit of info that communicates more meaningfully about "me" than the information in the first paragraph. I am (I presume like you) passionate about what I do. I love to teach, guide, mentor, learn, supervise, and lead. For me, leadership is self-preservation. Personally and professionally, I strive to do my very best, to use whatever God-given leadership talents I possess to make a difference in the lives of others. I continually strive to improve myself intellectually and socially, but also physically and spiritually. Family and community are very important to me. Building and sustaining community is integral to my professional practice. I see myself as part of a larger community of learners as we share, experience, overcome difficulties, learn from our mistakes, and in the end help others (students, colleagues, and community members) achieve their educational goals.

If any of the information in this book series touches you in any way, please feel free to contact me by using my personal e-mail address: tora.dojo@verizon.net. I encourage you to share your reactions, comments, and suggestions, or simply to relate an anecdote or two, humorous or otherwise, that may serve as "information from the field" for future editions of this work, ultimately to help others. Your input is much appreciated.

Questionnaire: Before We Get Started . . .

D *irections:* Using the Likert scale below, circle the answer that best represents your on-the-spot belief about each statement. The questionnaire serves as an advanced organizer of sorts for some of the key topics in this book, although items are purposely constructed in no particular order. Discussion of each topic, though, occurs within the context of relevant chapters. Responses or views to each statement are presented in a subsection following the questionnaire (this section begins "Now, let's analyze your responses . . ."). You may or may not agree with the points made, but I hope you will be encouraged to reflect on your own views. Reflective activities follow to allow for deeper analysis. Elaboration of ideas emanating from this brief activity will occur throughout the text and series. I encourage you to share reflections (yours and mine) with colleagues. I'd appreciate your personal feedback via the e-mail address I've listed in the "About the Author" section.

SA = Strongly Agree ("For the most part, yes.")

A = Agree ("Yes, but . . .")

D = Disagree ("No, but . . .")

SD = Strongly Disagree ("For the most part, no.")

SA   A   D   SD   1. Since I am so busy with in-school affairs, I really cannot devote the time to build strong, enduring relations with the community, other than with parents of course.

SA A D SD   2. I think I should devote most, if not all, of my time working with teachers on promoting good teaching practice in order to promote student achievement. Dealing with noninstructional, community-related issues is simply distracting and would have, in the end, a dubious impact on student learning.

SA A D SD   3. Principals are expected to do it all; we simply cannot. Hold us accountable for those areas we can impact. As for community relations, it's a waste of time.

SA A D SD   4. I acknowledge my responsibility for organizing and implementing an effective school-community relations program.

SA A D SD   5. I sincerely believe that my involvement in building community relations will have a very positive effect on student learning. We cannot simply abrogate our responsibility to doing all we can to promote student achievement.

SA A D SD   6. If we do not actively campaign to forge meaningful school-community relations, our ability to help children succeed academically will be limited.

SA A D SD   7. One of my most important responsibilities is to reach out to parents in meaningful and sustained ways.

SA A D SD   8. I actively seek to engage parents in school governance and decision-making authority in my school.

SA A D SD   9. Building a strong public relations program is essential to my school's success.

SA A D SD   10. I spend a good portion of my week forging community alliances in order to support what we do in school.

SA A D SD   11. I actively campaign for select local politicians because they play an important role in sustaining vital community relations activities.

SA A D SD   12. We educators do not work hard enough to narrow the black-white achievement gap. We can indeed do more and work harder to eliminate such differences in academic achievement.

SA A D SD   13. I play an important role in closing the black-white achievement gap.

SA A D SD   14. Whole school reform necessitates our involvement in and commitment to school-community relations.

SA A D SD   15. I need to do more to build and sustain a sound school-community relations program.

Before we analyze your responses, consider the fact that our beliefs influence our actions and, more specifically, our commitment to school-community relations. Do you really believe that the time spent on nurturing community relations is in fact time well spent? If so, how much time would you allot? Also, if you do support community involvement, to what extent do you do this? This work will emphasize a rather vigorous commitment to school-community relations that many principals may find overwhelming. Without a firm belief that such work will make a difference to both school morale and, ultimately, student achievement, a principal is not likely to commit the time and energy necessary to make school-community work effective. Examine the premises that follow to determine your commitment to school-community work. Do the following ideas and activities match your own sense of how you see yourself involved in such work?

A school-community leader

- envisions the school building as nested within a larger community structure;
- considers ways the school may meet community needs and vice versa;
- realizes that external community factors may influence student learning even more than what goes on in school;
- spends much time forging and sustaining relations with parents, certainly, but also with local business people, religious institutions, social and health agencies, and civic groups;
- thinks creatively about different ways of involving others in school matters;
- shares information with community partners;
- listens to community partners about ways of improving the school or suggestions for further collaborations;
- encourages innovative ideas and thinking by all members of the community;
- forms committees of internal and external constituents to plan strategically about ways to improve the school, in general, and more specifically, ways of better promoting student achievement.

As you consider the meaning and relevance of school-community leadership, share your thoughts about these questions with a colleague:

Reflective Questions

1. Do you really believe school-community relations are essential to your work as principal? How so? Be specific.

2. How much time would you devote to forging such relationships? With all that you do, how would you find the time to build community ties to your school?

3. How would you utilize parents in your school?

4. What does school-community leadership mean to you, and why is it so important, if it is? Explain.

5. What are specific ways you solicit community collaboration in your school?

6. What school-community practices or programs have you seen that really work well? Share with a colleague.

* * * * * * * * * * * * * * * *

Examine these quotations on school-community relations. What do they mean to you?

"The move to community-building in education . . . reflects a growing awareness of the profound need . . . to feel part of something larger than themselves."

—Rachel Kessler

"One of the biggest problems of schools is that they have pulled themselves away from the public. There cannot be a border between the school and the community, where the school ends the community starts."

—Rod Paige

"[Democratic society] must have a type of education which gives individuals a personal interest in social relationships and control, and the habits of mind which secure social change without introducing disorder."

—John Dewey

"The school exists for and serves the community."

—James Scheurich

"Where the importance of parental involvement is explicit in the research, the importance of community involvement is more implicit."

—Robert J. Marzano

* * * * * * * * * * * * * * * *

Now, let's analyze your responses to the questionnaire:

1. Since I am so busy with in-school affairs, I really cannot devote the time to build strong, enduring relations with the community, other than with parents of course.

Principals today cannot afford to take such stands. Schools are so complex today that inattention to concrete and sensible ways to involve community to benefit the school is shortsighted at best. Certainly, you are quite busy with a plethora of demands within your school building. Still, without serious and mindful attention to building school-community ties, you will not be able to best and most effectively address the varied needs of learners in your building. Without doubt, principals should establish leadership practices that consider the importance of involving school district and community resources in order to further the school's mission. Your effectiveness as a principal is contingent on your ability to reign in community-wide resources aimed at enhancing the educational experiences of students and directly or indirectly promoting student learning. Your work in schools does not occur, and must not occur, in isolation from the large external school community (Epstein et al., 2002).

2. I think I should devote most, if not all, of my time working with teachers on promoting good teaching practice in order to promote student achievement. Dealing with noninstructional, community-related issues is simply distracting and would have, in the end, a dubious impact on student learning.

Certainly some could argue by citing relevant research (e.g., Leithwood, Seashore Louis, Anderson, & Wahlstrom, 2004; Marzano, Pickering, & Pollock, 2001) that working directly with teachers on instructional matters has significant positive consequences for student learning. However, given the complex nature of teaching and learning, combined with many outside school influences on student learning, careful attention to factors beyond the classroom and even the school door can only bring to bear additional important resources to assist in our work as principals. Of course, most of our efforts should involve utilizing community resources that have a direct impact in the classroom. For instance, if a local senator's office can provide a modest $20,000 grant to purchase a dozen or so extra computers along with wireless capability and other multimedia items, then teachers would have better resources to accomplish their ultimate goal of promoting student achievement. Successful principals look for creative ways outside the four walls of the school to enhance instructional and curricular work within the school building. These principals make a difference because they are forward-looking, optimistic, and will do almost anything to further the school mission. Studying the work of noteworthy principals will indicate that they do not find noninstructional, community-related issues as distracting, but on the contrary, they are aware that such efforts and resources accumulated might just make the difference (e.g., Goldberg, 2001).

3. Principals are expected to do it all; we simply cannot. Hold us accountable for those areas we can impact. As for community relations, it's a waste of time.

The public certainly expects much from principals. Still, many realize that principals cannot indeed do it alone. But to negate obligations to connect to the community is shortsighted, if not incompetent. It is in fact because principals cannot accomplish their objectives without the assistance of others that they reach out to important community members and agencies in relevant and meaningful ways. Principals should be accountable to establish connections with the community in order to channel resources that might not otherwise be available to schools. These resources, personnel or otherwise, might make the difference. Is this difficult work? Indeed. Is it a "waste of time?" Most definitely not.

4. I acknowledge my responsibility for organizing and implementing an effective school-community relations program.

Community relations leadership is not a luxury or optional. It is a moral imperative for 21st-century principals. You must take a proactive stance by articulating a commitment toward establishing contacts with the community to better promote student achievement. Then, you must take specific measures to reach out to the community. Developing a plan, strategic or otherwise, is recommended. Effective school-community leaders undertake the following, among other, activities:

- *Visit local business establishments.*
- *Call on local health agencies.*
- *Join local civic associations.*
- *Participate in nonschool community functions.*
- *Conduct ongoing parent workshops.*
- *Attract parent and community volunteers to the school.*
- *Organize student and parent events.*
- *Solicit partnerships with local colleges.*
- *Celebrate community events.*
- *Circulate school-community newsletters.*
- *Host community breakfasts.*
- *Foster a welcoming environment conducive to collaboration and involvement.*

Fiore (2002) suggests that you create a school-community relations plan. He offers three kinds of plans:

- *The Coordinated Plan—A plan developed by the school with representatives from the community. "A coordinated school-community relations plan that is organized and carried out effectively offers an excellent opportunity for cooperation and consistency with a school system" (p. 15). Although the principal retains authority, involvement of central office staff and other community nonprofessional educators is vital to its success.*

- *The Centralized Plan—These plans are initiated and coordinated by central office staff, usually by the superintendent or designee. The advantage of such a plan centers on tapping into central office personnel's vast expertise and resources relating to public relations and community involvement. "Many argue that although the superintendent may know the larger community well, the building level administrators best understand the populations served by each individual school" (p. 16).*

- *The Decentralized Plan*—*This plan involves almost no direct participation of the central office. Authority for development and coordination rests with the building principal. "The common belief is that the principal is in the best position to develop a school-community relations plan that will be of the most benefit to his or her own particular school" (p. 17). Depending on your experience, such a plan allows a principal to frame a community effort that meets the specific needs of a particular school.*

Fiore (2002) cautions that "There are pros and cons to all three types of plans. . . . [Ultimately], it is the principal's responsibility to develop and maintain positive relationships with the school-community—both internally and externally" (p. 17). Fiore provides an easy-to-refer-to checklist of questions to consider whenever framing such a plan:

- *Does the plan make use of appropriate and varied communication channels for the various audiences involved?*
- *Do all individuals with responsibility in the school-community relations plan know what the goals and objectives are?*
- *Does the plan contain strategies for involving all stakeholder groups whenever possible?*
- *Are the goals, objectives, and desired outcomes of the school-community relations plan consistent with the school philosophy and the state's laws?*
- *Are the goals, objectives, and desired outcomes stated in measurable terms to the extent possible?*
- *Has the design of the plan's strategies and activities considered available human resources, funds, and facilities?*
- *Does the plan distinguish between long- and short-term goals and objectives?*
- *Are there provisions in the plan for future audits of its effectives and results?*
- *Is the school-community relations plan tailored to the specific needs of the school and its community?*
- *Does the school-community relations plan take into account the need for in-service education of the staff? (p. 14)*

5. I sincerely believe that my involvement in building community relations will have a very positive effect on student learning.

We cannot simply abrogate our responsibility to doing all we can to promote student achievement.

Promoting student achievement is undoubtedly our number one objective. Good principals utilize a multifaceted approach to build and sustain a sound learning community that supports good teaching and high achievement for all students. These principals realize that many complex factors affect learning. In-school and out-of-school factors play critical roles. Direct and indirect approaches are needed. Although instructional leadership is now widely viewed as most critical for principals, creating learning communities that include "educators, students, parents, and community partners who work together to improve the school and enhance students' learning opportunities" (Epstein & Salinas, 2004, p. 12) is equally essential.

6. If we do not actively campaign to forge meaningful school-community relations, our ability to help children succeed academically will be limited.

The answer to this item reaffirms the belief previously described.

7. One of my most important responsibilities is to reach out to parents in meaningful and sustained ways.

I've personally never met a principal who would not solicit parental involvement in student learning at least, in some way. Allow me to relate a humorous but true incident when I was asked at a job interview if I was committed to parental involvement. I didn't want them (a committee comprised of administrators, teachers, and parents) to forget my response, which hopefully captured my commitment to parents. I rose out of my seat, taking a marker and pad in hand, and said:

"Let me show you what I mean when I say that parental involvement is essential." I held up a blank piece of paper (Figure 1). I continued, "Within a school there are basically three groups of individuals. There are faculty (including administration and teachers), there are students, and there are parents (i.e., community)." As I mentioned each group, I drew a small oval until I developed the configuration seen in Figure 2. "Quite often," I lamented, "when faculty work on their side, and the parents work on their side, all without partnership and commitment, the students are left in the middle." As I mentioned "the faculty," I placed a dot in

the center of the left-hand oval; as I mentioned "the parents," I placed a dot in the center of the right-hand oval; and as I mentioned "the students," I merely pointed to the center oval. I ended up with the configuration in Figure 3.

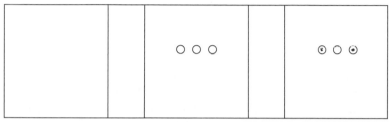

| Figure 1 | Figure 2 | Figure 3 |

"When this happens," I continued, "when there is no communication and teamwork between these two sides, the whole system can get looking pretty unhappy." As I said, "when there is no communication," I drew the curved line under the three ovals. The configuration now resembled the sad face shown in Figure 4.

Figure 4

"But, let's add teamwork. Let's get everyone working together to help our children. When parents and faculty work together constructively, the whole school is unified." As I mentioned "working together," I drew a large encompassing oval around the sad face so that it looked like Figure 5.

SOURCE: Illustrations from Mamchak, P. Susan, and Mamchak, Steven R., *School Administrator's Public Speaking Portfolio.* (c) Jossey-Bass. Reprinted with permission of John Wiley & Sons, Inc.

Figure 5

"Then," I concluded, "thanks to teamwork and spirit of coopera-
tiveness, students will succeed and we will have a happy and functioning school; one we may all be justly proud of." As I said the last
words, I turned the drawing around 180 degrees. Before the eyes of
the committee, it turned into the happy face as seen in Figure 6.

Figure 6

Although this was a somewhat contrived and simple demonstra-
tion of my philosophical commitment to parental involvement,
several committee members did smile, and I'm certain I effectively
communicated my point. Involve parents in any way possible. Here
are some suggestions:

1. Invite their participation on needs assessment and goal
committees through formal and informal invitations.

2. Sponsor an open house at which you will provide refreshments and outline the nature of participation you desire.

3. Develop a parent hotline so that parents may be kept abreast
of "what's happenin'" in the school.

4. Invite parents to a parent-student picture night.

Now, commitment to parental involvement may be contrived or
sincere. You'll need to determine that for yourself. But even if you are

sincere, what is the nature of such involvement? Do you believe that parents are important only in working with their child at home on homework and school-related projects? Or, would you also invite parents to join in-school curriculum committees, or even contribute to shared decision making? Reaching out to parents is one thing; the nature of that involvement is quite another.

8. I actively seek to engage parents in school governance and decision-making authority in my school.

Picking up from the response to the last item, would you in fact engage parents in such meaningful activities and responsibilities? One of the major responsibilities of school-community leadership is engaging parents in significant and ongoing involvement in all aspects of the school programming. As Buchen (2003) observes, "Parents are taking more assertive roles, moving well beyond the stereotype of running bake sales" (p. 46). Successful principal school-community leaders engage in the following, among others, parent-related activities:

- *Invite parents to join a variety of school and curriculum-related committees.*
- *Provide parent area, with parent resources.*
- *Solicit their advice for better ways of conducting school business.*
- *Identify their professional expertise in order to involve them in your school in some creative way.*
- *Share your ideas with them.*
- *Establish ongoing educational and social workshops for them.*
- *Ask them to conduct relevant workshops matched to their areas of interest and expertise.*
- *Ask them to volunteer to read to or tutor children.*
- *Involve them in action research projects.*
- *Let them serve as school representatives at various community social or cultural functions.*
- *Involve them in recruitment initiatives.*
- *Include them in school governance.*

9. Building a strong public relations program is essential to my school's success.

Here is another area that some principals may not think about. Successful principals think out of the box . . . and out of the school for that matter. How might promoting in-school affairs to the public at large assist you in accomplishing your educational objectives? Highlighting innovative school projects might, for instance, attract the attention of some business or private enterprise that might, in turn, want to donate some funds to expand the project. Computer companies often look out for their own public relations (PR) interests and would be willing to donate some new technologies. Private individuals, especially alumni, might take interest in that project by donating special funds to support school-related initiatives. Here are some ways principals might initiate a PR campaign:

- *Form a PR campaign committee comprised of teachers, administrators, students, parents, and a nonparent community member if possible.*
- *Develop a strategic plan with listed objectives and concrete strategies for initiation.*
- *Create a newsletter for community-wide distribution that highlights monthly school projects, latest announcements, teacher achievements, and so on.*
- *Get out into the community on a weekly basis to herald school achievements (e.g., visit local stores and agencies, have lunch or dinner with key community officials and even politicians).*
- *Publish relevant statistics that either highlight school successes or list suggestions for potential donors to assist needed areas (e.g., technology, sports, curriculum resources).*

10. I spend a good portion of my week forging community alliances in order to support what we do in school.

"Good portion" is key. I would say that "quality" time is more important than "quantity." A strong school-community leader does not sit behind the desk, but pays close attention to community activities. Ongoing visits and engagements within the community are warranted. Schedule, at the very least, monthly meetings with key community members (e.g., lunch with the local Rotary Club). Join local associations and participate actively.

11. I actively campaign for select local politicians because they play an important role in sustaining vital community relations activities.

Caution here is suggested. Interacting with local politicians is wise, but given the vicissitudes of politics and the ever-changing nature of alliances, siding with one politician over another might come back to bite you, so to speak. Maintaining friendly relations to all is highly recommended. As principal of a school, your advocacy of one person over another carries some weight. Always consult your superintendent for advice before you engage in a political campaign. From my experience, politicians will be willing to assist your school-related projects regardless of your personal political stance. Seize on their willingness to help.

12. We educators do not work hard enough to narrow the black-white achievement gap. We can indeed do more and work harder to eliminate such differences in academic achievement.

We are too insular in our approach to raising academic achievement, especially in regard to the so-called black-white achievement gap. We must realize that many non–school-related forces and factors affect student achievement. Although we must remain cognizant of our responsibilities to promote student learning within our direct areas of control, proactive school-community leaders attempt to influence non–school-related factors that also impact student learning. Principals can contribute greatly to the larger effort to narrow this achievement gap by serving as advocates, for example, of "policies to stabilize family housing, school-community health clinics, early childhood education, after school programs, and summer programs" (Levine, 2004, p. xi).

13. I play an important role in closing the black-white achievement gap.

Effective school-community leaders exude a confident, optimistic belief that their work makes a difference. A high sense of efficacy characterizes these individuals. As principal, you remain committed to the notion that all students can learn, albeit at different rates and in different ways. You are unrelenting in pursuit of ways to help each child succeed and reach his or her potential. Although you are aware of the practical limits of your efforts, you remain steadfast to your commitment to reducing, if not closing, the achievement gap.

14. Whole school reform necessitates our involvement in and commitment to school-community relations.

Much has been written about whole school reform (e.g., Elmore, 1999; Fullan, 1999). Enormous energies and efforts have been expended on alternative ways of structuring schools, modifying curricula, and providing additional instructional resources that support student learning.

Federal legislation (i.e., the No Child Left Behind Act of 2002) has made a significant mark on American education. Although pockets of success stories exist, little change has been effected on a systemic or schools-wide basis. As alluded to earlier, educators should remain cognizant of ways they may influence out-of-the-school factors that affect student learning. Although they cannot, by themselves, create sustained whole school improvement (a societal effort is needed, as will be argued at greater length later in this volume), they do play, especially we principals, a significant influential role. The more you consider and act on school-community initiatives, the better position you'll be in to effect changes in your school that you might not otherwise be able to accomplish. An important reason for our involvement in school-community relations is to somehow have an impact on whole school reform by utilizing resources external to the school building that may just make the difference.

15. I need to do more to build and sustain a sound school-community relations program.

Self-assessment here is critical. In writing this book, I interviewed several current principals. Except for one, each reported a commitment to school-community relations but said that "I could/should be doing much more." Hopefully this book will encourage your continued efforts in this area.

Reflective Questions

1. Which of the explanations above make the most sense to you?

2. Which of the explanations above make the least sense to you? Explain why.

3. Can you think of an instance when you were involved in a meaningful school-relations venture or project? Describe the project, your involvement, what you learned, and how the experience befitted student learning.

4. Can you think of principals who serve as exemplars in school-community relations? What qualities do they possess? Are such qualities replicable? What can you learn from them?

5. In what ways do you reach out to parents? Community representatives? Explain in detail.

6. Do you believe that your work can make a significant difference in the achievement of students in your school? What factors are in your control? What factors are beyond your control? Is there any way to influence some of those factors you currently feel are beyond your control? Explain. What must society or other agencies do to assist? How might you utilize community resources to facilitate the process?

See Resource B for a more detailed survey to assess your role as a school-community leader.

C H A P T E R   O N E

Introduction

"The entire school territory—the community—is involved in the process of education. . . . Communication between parents and other citizens, businesses, health and social care agencies, several levels of government, teachers, administrators, and students is essential and is the glue that binds the learning community."

—Gerald C. Ubben,
Larry W. Hughes, and Cynthia J. Norris

"Clearly, more needs to be done to encourage principals to make the most of potential community contributions to student learning. By building partnerships with existing agencies and groups within the community, school leaders can enhance student achievement and success by creating learning communities that have access to resources beyond those within the school."

—Peter Gretz

"Many recent polls conducted by various school administrator associations . . . rated school-community relations as the first or second most important aspect of their job."

—Douglas J. Fiore

T homas Sergiovanni (1995) defines community as

collections of people bonded together by mutual commitments and special relationships, who together are bound to a set of shared ideas and values that they believe in, and feel compelled to follow. This bonding and binding helps them to become members of a tightly knit web of meaningful relationships and moral overtones. In communities of this kind, people belong, people care, people help each other, people make and keep commitments, people feel responsible for themselves and responsible to others. (p. 100)

School-community leadership, at its best, fosters such relationships. Principals don't simply mouth platitudes about community but rather are involved in ongoing, deep community partnerships that ultimately and most importantly support student learning.

According to Starratt and Howells (1998), "schools as communities have two purposes. One is the promotion of quality academic learning for all students. The second is the socialization of the group into the experience and practice of the community itself" (p. 1000). Although enhancing student learning is first and foremost, several other benefits accrue:

- Student acculturation into community
- Community understanding of school needs
- Staff viewed as community partners
- Parents participate in school and community affairs
- Schools seen as integral part of a larger community

Some principals get so bogged down in managing their school they forget the importance of reaching out to the community to forge those bonds that Sergiovanni explained above. As an effective school-community leader, your role and responsibility does not end at the school door. You realize that there are community forces that impinge on your activities in the school building. Expectations for leadership in the community abound. You utilize the community as a resource but also as an essential partner in furthering the school mission.

As you build educational partnerships, you will intentionally utilize community resources to improve your school. David Sadker and Myra Sadker (2000, p. 346) categorize community resources into nine major categories:

1. Professional associations (e.g., architects, lawyers, and engineers)

2. Environmental and conservation organizations

3. Museums, galleries, and other cultural attractions

4. Social and civic groups (e.g., League of Women Voters, Rotary and Lions clubs, historical societies, YMCA, Boy/ Girl Scouts, fraternities and sororities)

5. Colleges and universities

6. Ethnic and cultural groups

7. Health agencies and hospitals

8. Senior citizens

9. Artists, musicians, and craftspeople

Certainly, the greatest and most available community resource at your disposal is the parent. As principal, you should carefully consider the nature and extent of parental involvement in your school. Cotton (2003) reports that "it is not surprising to learn that principals of high-achieving schools are more involved in outreach to parents and other community members than are less-successful principals" (p. 18). Research also demonstrates that higher-achieving schools have greater parent satisfaction (Davis, 1998). What do such principals do?

- Share their vision of best practice with parents at every turn.
- Invite community leaders to school functions.
- Invite parents as classroom helpers.
- Hold meetings and forums in local places of worship, community centers, etc.
- Use the school itself as a community center.
- Attend central office meetings.

- Conduct workshops for parents and other interested community members.
- Solicit input from parents and community leaders about school decisions.
- Get out of their office.

Discovering natural and creative ways to reach out to parents is imperative for the principal as school-community leader.

This book represents one aspect of a principal's work. Each book in the series addresses a specific, important role or function of a principal. Discussing each separately, however, is quite artificial and a bit contrived. In fact, all seven forms of leadership (instructional, cultural, ethical/spiritual, collaborative, operational, strategic, and school-community) form an undifferentiated whole. Still, we can glean much from a more in-depth analysis of each form of leadership. It is with such understanding that this book is framed. School-community leadership reflects an educational paradigm based on the following assumptions or premises:

- You, as principal, play the most vital role to facilitate (i.e., establish and sustain) ongoing, meaningful, and effective school-community relations. In fact, without your commitment and efforts, little will be accomplished regarding community-school involvement.
- Schools are too complex and the needs so enormous that to exclude assistance from others in the community is shortsighted.
- Planned and organized engagement of parents is imperative both at home and at school.
- Parental involvement has a very positive effect on high achievement for all students.
- Principals encourage wide community participation in school affairs to the extent that such involvement promotes, directly or indirectly, student learning.
- Schools cannot improve without the systematic and ongoing participation of many individuals (see, e.g., Glanz & Sullivan, 2000).

Many schools engage parents and community but few have articulated, well-developed strategic plans linked to school goals and a mission that provides ongoing, in-depth attention to school-community relations. Such an observation reflects Epstein and Salinas's (2004) conception of partnering with families and communities. They state, "Many schools conduct at least a few activities to involve families in their children's education, but most do not have well-organized, goal-linked, and sustainable partnership programs" (p. 18).

Reflective Questions

1. Consider leaders you have known. Assess their school-community leadership skills. What stands out as particularly noteworthy? Unworthy?

2. Assess the degree to which a "true school-community spirit" exists in your school. How can you contribute to a more involved and spirited community outreach program?

3. What school-community leadership challenges do you face? Explain.

4. React to the assumptions listed above. Which make the most sense to you?

5. What is the benefit of a school-community plan? Describe a school in which such a plan exists.

---

* * * * * * * * * * * * * * *

The major themes of this book and series on the principalship are as follows:

- The principal models school-community leadership in all aspects of school work.
- The success of a school-community effort rests with the principal.
- Parental involvement is the most essential element of any school-community relations program.
- Building school-community alliances takes time, but the benefits are immeasurable.
- Principals and schools cannot by themselves solve all students' instructional problems as other factors come into play (e.g., socioeconomic, health).

- Yet, principals do a play a role in facilitating whole school reform by encouraging attention to these out-of-school factors.
- School-community relations can affect student achievement.

This book and series are also aligned with standards established by the prominent Educational Leadership Constituent Council (ELCC). ELCC standards are commonly accepted by most educational organizations concerned with preparing high-quality educational leaders and as such are most authoritative (Wilmore, 2002). The ELCC, an arm of the National Council for the Accreditation of Teacher Education (NCATE), developed six leadership standards used widely in principal preparation. These standards form the basis for this book and series:

1.0: Candidates who complete the program are educational leaders who have the knowledge and ability to promote the success of all students by facilitating the development, articulation, implementation, and stewardship of a school or district vision of learning supported by the school community.

2.0: Candidates who complete the program are educational leaders who have the knowledge and ability to promote the success of all students by promoting a positive school culture, providing an effective instructional program, applying best practices to student learning, and designing comprehensive professional growth plans for staff.

3.0: Candidates who complete the program are educational leaders who have the knowledge and ability to promote the success of all students by managing the organization, operations, and resources in a way that promotes a safe, efficient, and effective learning environment.

**4.0: Candidates who complete the program are educational leaders who have the knowledge and ability to promote the success of all students by collaborating with families and other community members, responding to diverse community interests and needs, and mobilizing community resources.

5.0: Candidates who complete the program are educational leaders who have the knowledge and ability to promote the success of all students by acting with integrity, fairly, and in an ethical manner.

6.0: Candidates who complete the program are educational leaders who have the knowledge and ability to promote the success of all students by understanding, responding to, and influencing the larger political, social, economic, legal, and cultural context.

** This standard is addressed in this book.

Readers should also familiarize themselves with Interstate School Leaders Licensure Consortium (ISLLC) and National Association of Elementary School Principals (NAESP) standards (see, e.g., http://www.ccsso.org/projects/Interstate_School_Leaders_Licensure_Consortium/ and http://www.boyercenter.org/basicschool/naesp.shtml).

You may think that school-community leadership may not have as immediate a payback as some other forms of leadership. However, underestimating the long-range impact of school-community leadership is shortsighted. Marshalling community resources can have direct and indirect influences on school improvement and, more specifically, on student learning.

Reflective Questions

1. Which of the themes above make the most sense to you?

2. Which of the themes above make the least sense to you? Explain.

3. How do you perceive your role as school-community leader? What specific actions must you take to be effective? Be specific.

4. What do you do on a daily basis that affirms your commitment to school-community leadership? Provide detailed examples.

5. How do school-community relations affect student achievement, directly or indirectly? Be specific.

---

* * * * * * * * * * * * * * *

In order to establish a framework for the three main chapters, Figure 1.1 illustrates the role of the principal attempting to facilitate and influence the critical elements of school-community relations (i.e., encouraging parent involvement, building community alliances, and affecting out-of-school factors that affect student learning). Effective principals reach out to a variety of community constituents. When these aspects of school-community relations work at their best, a large array of forces, resources, and personnel are brought to bear to positively influence student achievement.

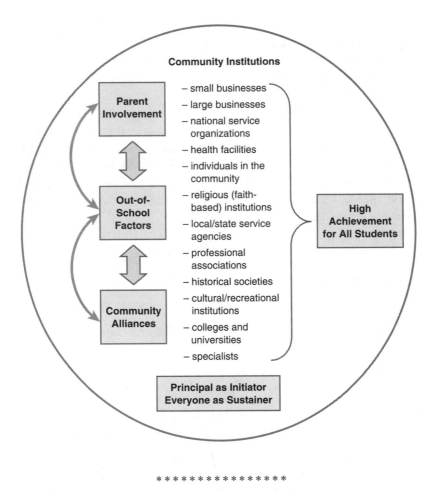

* * * * * * * * * * * * * * * *

Allow me to offer a word on chapter format and presentation of information. Information in Chapters 2 through 4 is presented as concisely as possible to make for easy and quick reference reading. Each chapter begins with boxed material called "What You Should Know About." The box will list and briefly explain the concepts covered in each chapter. Certainly, each chapter will not cover every bit of information there is to know about a given topic, as mentioned earlier. Each chapter culls, though, essential knowledge, skills, and dispositions necessary for a successful principal.

A brief word on chapter organization is in order to facilitate reading. Chapter 2 includes some best practices for reaching out to parents, so critical for any school-community initiative. After reviewing some practical strategies, obvious and not so obvious ones, Chapter 3 highlights practices for establishing a variety of community alliances that support school initiatives. Chapter 4 addresses the most critical problem of ensuring high achievement for all students, black and white. School-community leadership must be aimed at using community resources and reforms that promote learning for all students. Involvement in community merely for the sake of public relations is insufficient. Efforts must always be geared to strengthen collaborations that are aimed to help children learn; that's the bottom line for any form of school leadership. Taken together, these three chapters provide you with information and strategies that promote a sense of community involvement. This book is not meant to be the definitive treatise on school-community leadership, but rather to raise some relevant issues for your consideration. It is my hope that the ideas in this book will give you pause to think about your own role in community relations.

As a concluding activity to this Introduction, read the boxed material below that contains 11 quotations meant to inspire but more importantly to provoke critical thinking about your role as school-community leader. Read each quotation and ask yourself these questions:

- What does the author convey about collaboration, directly or indirectly (in other words, what's the message in a nutshell)?
- Critique the quotation. Does the thought reflect your beliefs? Explain.
- What practical step(s) could you take to actualize the idea behind each quotation?

Some Key Quotations
Related to School-Community Leadership

"We need to surround kids with adults who know and care for our children, who have opinions and are accustomed to expressing them publicly, and who know how to reach reasonable collective decisions in the face of disagreement. That means increasing local decision making and simultaneously decreasing the size and bureaucratic complexity of schools."

—Deborah Meier

"[We need a] . . . critically imaginative vision that sees leadership as a community effort to redesign schools for the maximization of the interest of that community for the school is not simply an organizational complex, with function and structure, peopled by workers exercising some status or role."

—Spencer Maxcy

"Nothing is more important to our shared future than the well being of children. For the children are at our core—not only as vulnerable beings in need of love and care but as a moral touchstone amidst the complexity and contentiousness of modern life. Just as it takes a village to raise a child, it takes children to raise up a village to become all it should be. The village we build with them in mind will be a better place for us all."

—Hillary Rodham Clinton

"If we really believe family/community involvement is linked to student success, we must stop giving lip service and allocate at least modest sums for staff development, outreach, and coordination of activities."

—Nancy Feyl Chavkin

"In many communities, partnerships involving schools and other community organizations and agencies are addressing . . . challenges. Such partnerships are helping to create community schools that offer supports and opportunities to enable all children and youth to learn and succeed and to help families and communities thrive.

These partnerships are enhancing the core mission of schools: improving academic achievement."

—Anonymous (*NASSP Bulletin*)

"Schools [should] develop public relations strategies to inform families, businesses, and the community about family/community involvement policies and programs through newsletters, slide shows, videotapes, local newspapers, and other media. It is critical that the strategies recognize the importance of a community's historical, ethnic, linguistic, and cultural resources."

—Nancy Feyl Chavkin

"By the year 2000, every school will promote partnerships that will increase parental involvement and participation in promoting the social, emotional, and academic growth of children."

—GOALS 2000

"The same sensitivity required for shaping culture internally must be applied to linking the school to parents and other members of the community."

—Terrence E. Deal and Kent D. Peterson

"It is false to claim that higher standards, more testing and accountability, and better school leadership can close the achievement gap. . . . They may be able to narrow it some; by how much remains to be determined."

—Richard Rothstein

"Rather than waste so much time arguing . . . , policy makers, business and community leaders, and educators must learn to work together in new ways to 'reinvent' the American education system so that all students can find both challenge and joy in learning."

—Tony Wagner

"All teachers should be involved in their communities not just because of the obvious reasons but also because of the political ramifications. . . . PR work is needed to demonstrate the many services that a school provides and the good things that occur there."

—John G. Gabriel

CASE STUDY* AND REFLECTIVE QUESTIONS

The Oakridge Public School District is located in a suburban setting approximately 80 miles north of New York City. The regional population is approximately 250,000. For a suburban area, however, it has attracted a relatively high percentage of industries and commercial establishments, probably due to its lower tax base. Within a 10-mile radius, three institutions of higher learning are available. The Oakridge School District, although not particularly diverse, is committed to preparing students to live in a culturally diverse and global society. The district maintains a strong commitment to educational excellence and community involvement.

When the earthquake and resulting tsunami that wrecked coastlines along the Indian Ocean and killed an estimated 250,000 people hit, James McGregor, principal of Oakridge Middle School, seized the moment by planning a community-wide effort to raise awareness of the tragedy, which would include recruiting students in his school to play an active role in the relief effort. Wanting to use the catastrophic opportunity as a learning experience, Principal McGregor contacted several lead teachers during the Christmas break to solicit their involvement in planning curricular and instructional activities when students returned. Teachers, under his facilitative leadership, designed lessons and assembly programs. Flags at the school were flown at half-staff to honor the dead, plans were made to raise money for relief efforts, and science and social studies teachers decided to engage students in lessons to help them understand the natural disaster and its long-term implications for human welfare.

Susan Fearson, a science teacher at the 900-student Oakridge Middle School, engaged students in such topics as energy transfer, plate tectonics, and the way in which waves travel. "It was an invaluable opportunity to bring science they have learned into events that were happening in the world," she said. She had her students spend a day reading articles she had collected from newspapers and the Internet. The next day, they created a timeline on a world map showing how the disaster unfolded. They also wrote one-page essays on different aspects of the tsunami.

In social studies, Chester Esser said the best way to teach about the disaster is to link it to something the students are already learning or

---

* This case study has been developed from information gleaned from Trotter, A., Honawar, V., & Tonn, J. L. (2005, January 12). U.S. schools find lessons in tsunami. *Education Week, 24*(18), 1, 2.

already know. For example, he engaged students in research and discussions about how the natural catastrophe might affect existing conflicts in Sri Lanka and on the Indonesian island of Sumatra.

Principal McGregor invited a local politician to speak to students at the school about the importance of the relief effort. Students were given a larger political and social context for the work they were about to undertake. The principal invited others from the community to share their views on how the community might come together during this momentous and tragic occasion.

Beyond these important instructional activities, Principal McGregor mobilized fund-raising efforts by calling together student, faculty, and staff leaders at the same time as he reached out to local businesses and corporations. In-school and community functions were rapidly coordinated to hold events that would raise substantial monies for the relief effort. Donations were solicited from the entire school community and given to the Red Cross during a major assembly program at the school. The event was covered by local newspapers and media. One article read, "At Oakridge Middle School, students, teachers, administrators, parents, and the local community rally to support the tsunami relief effort. It shows what whole community involvement can accomplish." Principal McGregor explained, "Community involvement is integral to our institutional mission, so it was natural for us to immediately think 'community' as we began relief efforts and educational planning."

Principal McGregor, well versed with community agencies and resources, contacted well-known relief agencies, such as the American Red Cross, Save the Children, and Care USA. He requested information about fund-raising activities and solicited their assistance for his work at the school. These three organizations later became the recipients of over $29,000 in collected donations. Several months later, McGregor was given the Principal-of-the-Year award by the school district, in large measure, for his school-community leadership that resulted in far more funds for the relief effort than other schools in the region. Sylvia Smith, superintendent, praised McGregor by explaining, "James displayed extraordinary leadership on multiple levels. While all principals should be commended for their in-school instructional and curricular efforts to engage students, he rose above the rest through community involvement on a massive scale. James is outstanding because of his articulated and actualized vision that it takes a whole community to educate children. We applaud his efforts and they serve to inspire all of us."

Reflective Questions

1. Why is James McGregor so committed to school-community leadership?

2. What makes his efforts so unique?

3. What educational benefits are there for student learning when schools engage with community?

4. What other activities would you have engaged in related to school-community involvement?

5. How might you demonstrate your commitment to school-community involvement?

6. In what ways can such efforts affect student learning and, ultimately, achievement?

As mentioned in the Introduction, Chapter 2 builds on the preceding information by highlighting some "best practices" for helping you create meaningful parental involvement so crucial for school-community leadership. These ideas are not meant to be exhaustive of the topic, but merely a means to encourage thinking related to "reaching out to parents."

CHAPTER TWO

Best Practices in Reaching Out to Parents

"Gone are the 'good old days' when educators were revered and respected for their wisdom and position by parents. . . . Today's parents are a different breed—less trusting of our educational platitudes and quick to point out what they perceive to be stupidity. . . . [Parents] resent being told to 'just trust us.'"

—Elaine K. McEwan

"Research shows that though students benefit modestly from having parents involved at school, what happens at home matters much more."

—Nancy Gibbs

"Research is accumulating that shows that particular parent involvement practices improve student achievement, attitudes, homework, report card grades, and aspirations."

—Joyce L. Epstein and Frances L. Van Voorhis

R esearch confirms that when schools reach out to families and communities, students do better in school on a range of social and academic indicators (Chavkin, 2000; Haynes & Emmons, 1997; Whitaker & Fiore, 2001). Henderson and Berla (1994, as cited by Gretz, 2003) explain that "students experience success when schools and families work together to support learning" (p. 32). I don't think that any reader will argue that parental involvement is unnecessary. Yet, one's commitment to the nature of that involvement will vary. As I noted in the Introduction, one of the major premises of this work is that engagement of parents is imperative both at home and at school. Effective principals engage in the following tasks, among others:

- Articulate a commitment to parental involvement
- Develop a strategic plan that addresses parental engagement in school
- Welcome parents at every opportunity (signs and posters in the school reflect such a welcoming message)
- Develop a close interpersonal and professional relationship with parents and the P.T.A.
- Provide ongoing, meaningful workshops for parents on varied topics of interest to both the school and parents
- Invite parents to join in-school committees (e.g., curriculum)
- Encourage shared decision-making experiences with parents on a host of relevant school-related issues
- Monitor parental involvement at home
- Survey parents' attitudes on a regular basis
- Provide ongoing communication

Reflective Questions

1. What is your commitment to parental involvement? Explain in depth.

2. In what specific areas or activities would you involve parents? Explain the nature and extent of this involvement.

3. In what specific areas or activities would you not involve them? Defend your position.

One of the other essential premises or assumptions of this work is that parental involvement that is targeted to promoting student achievement is most important. Swap (1993, as cited by Gretz, 2003) found that "parent involvement in students' education is directly related to children's achievement" (p. 32). Teachers, of course, play the single greatest role in school for promoting student learning (Leithwood, Seashore Louis, Anderson, & Wahlstrom, 2004). But if that is true, then parents are the single greatest influence of student learning at home. Effective schools and principals realize this fact but do not leave the nature and extent of this participation to chance. Effective principals realize they cannot do it alone. Parental engagement is imperative for student success, academically and socially. These proactive principals do their utmost to offer parents continued educational opportunities so that they too may serve as effective educators at home. In the current era of heightened accountability for student achievement, principal responsibility to do anything and everything to boost student achievement is more important than ever.

The work of Henderson and Mapp (2002) titled *A New Wave of Evidence: The Impact of School, Family and Community Connections on Student Achievement* is particularly insightful. Quoting the research published by the Southwest Educational Development Laboratory, the authors highlight specific academic-related benefits of parental involvement that include, among others,

> "A great school leader understands that parents are key partners in the education of their children."
>
> —Joel Klein

higher student grades and test scores, higher student enrollment in academic rigorous programs, higher high school graduation rates, lower dropout rates, higher attendance rates, and higher percentages of students who attend college. Some practical advice they give, relevant to you as a principal, includes the following points:

• Encourage face-to-face meetings whenever possible. Such involvement strengthens school-family communication and increases the likelihood that parents will attend school functions; it's also a time to discuss ways of best promoting student achievement.

• Communicate via e-mail and letter correspondence regularly. Some parents will prefer one method over another; do both. In your communications, always highlight the impor-

> *"The single most important aspect of a good parent/school/ community relationship is communication."*
>
> —Marcia Knoll

tance of achievement and how parents can assist. Give specific advice, avoiding generalities. For example, have parents say to their child, "Find a place at home you feel most comfortable to do your homework and let me know if you need my help," rather than just telling them to "try harder."

• Send learning (curricular and instructional) materials home. Make sure you include specific instructions for material use; just sending materials home without instructions might result in the materials sitting in the refuse pile at home.

• Keep parents informed about student progress. Don't just rely on report card time to communicate how a student is progressing. Regular and ongoing communiqués via e-mail, phone, in person, and letter will help to avoid surprises (e.g., "I had no idea Maria was having difficulty in science") and will involve parents throughout the school year in monitoring student work as well as providing academic guidance.

• Provide workshops on how parents can work with their child to promote achievement in reading, math, and other subjects. Providing parents with concrete and specific information, guidelines, and even techniques to teach their child at home will support teacher efforts in the classroom (e.g., teach parents how to effectively use "wait time" in working with their child at home).

Research has been conducted that demonstrates that high-performing schools exhibit similar characteristics involving community and school partnerships. Henderson and Mapp (2002) identify "three key practices" that are crucial in any school-community effort:

- Focus on building trusting, collaborative relationships among teachers, families, and community members. Good principals pay careful attention to building bridges between school and community. They seek opportunities to engage community members in school activities, but they also try to involve teachers and administrators in community functions outside of the school. Interest, legitimacy, and commitment are particularly affirmed when school people reach out to the community by actually attending community functions during or after school, and even on weekends. Trust and collaboration are important consequences of such engagements.

- Recognize, respect, and address families' needs, as well as class and cultural differences. Sincere concern for the family unit goes a long way toward cementing meaningful school-community relationships. Attempting to understand, for instance, unique cultural traditions of community members from diverse ethnicities indicates a willingness to listen and involve all members of the community. Culturally sensitive school practices are essential here.

> "When schools build partnerships with families that respond to their concerns, honor their contributions, and share power, they succeed in sustaining connections that are aimed at improving student achievement."
>
> —Anne T. Henderson and Karen L. Mapp

- Embrace a philosophy of partnership where power and responsibility are shared. High-performing schools involve parents and community members in significant school-related matters, not just bake sales. Your actions will speak louder than your words when you allow community members to participate in important school matters, instructional, curricular, or otherwise.

Schools are transformed when parents and the community are really involved. According to Henderson and Mapp (2002), recent studies have indicated that community involvement can result in these, among other, changes:

- Upgraded school facilities
- Improved school leadership and staffing
- Higher-quality learning programs for students
- New resources and programs to improve teaching and curriculum
- New funding for after-school programs and family supports

Reflective Questions

1. What is your reaction to the notion that parental involvement can improve student achievement? Explain the relationship between parental participation and student achievement.

2. What are the advantages and disadvantages of parent or community involvement?

3. Consider leaders you have known and know, and describe how they approach school-community leadership. What do they do that stands out in your mind? Would you call them school-community leaders? Explain why or why not.

The boxed material that follows summarizes the ideas highlighted in this chapter. The list is not exhaustive, but is merely meant to highlight some key concepts and ideas that successful school-community leaders should know about as they go about reaching out to parents. Please note that communities around the country are varied and represent different demographics, cultural differences, professional and organizational socialization patterns, and community expectations. Therefore, what may appear as a best practice in one community might be considered as a standard practice in another. These suggestions should be viewed within the frame that each school has unique and special circumstances.

The "best practices" highlighted in the remainder of this chapter are those that I have utilized in my practice as a school administrator, used in working closely with other principals, or culled from the research literature. Brief reflective activities follow each major concept to provoke thought on ways to implement and/or further understand each idea.

What You Should Know About Reaching Out to Parents

- **Learn Together**—We review Epstein and Salinas's "learning together" opportunities in school.
- **Empower Parents**—We review some of Lawrence-Lightfoot's recent research on parent-teacher relations.
- **Provide Training**—We review an idea once initiated in a school by Lester Kostick, a retired principal in New York.
- **Establish Parent Coordinators**—We review the institution of parent coordinator positions in New York City under the direction of School Chancellor Joel Klein.
- **Foster Parental Success**—We list Thompson's eight steps to parental success.
- **Publicize Student Presentations**—We discuss Fiore's suggestion of attracting parents via student presentations.
- **Solicit Parent and Community Involvement**—We look at Marzano's three research-based action steps to address community involvement.
- **Develop Parent Involvement Activities**—We mention Young's activities to encourage parent involvement.

---

1. LEARN TOGETHER

Epstein and Salinas (2004) distinguish between a "professional learning community" and a "school learning community." The former idea involves working primarily *in* the school to build strong, trusting professional relationships among teachers, administrators, and staff. Team-building activities are used to engender school spirit. This thinking is premised on the notion that such collaborative relationships will focus the group effort on improving student learning. Epstein and Salinas (2004) conclude, however, that such an approach "falls short of producing a true community of learners" (p. 12). In contrast, a school learning community "includes educators, students, parents, and community partners who work together to improve the school and enhance students' learning opportunities" (p. 12). Such efforts, according to these authors, are more enduring and comprehensive, especially when school and family partnerships are "linked to school goals" (p. 12). The best practice that follows may illustrate this approach.

A school-community leader does not view educators as the sole educational experts. As principal, you realize that, in the Deweyan sense, all of life educates. You see parents as true partners in your quest to help children learn and succeed. This notion doesn't infer that educators do not possess specific skills and information that can assist parents. Conversely, however, you realize that your success is based, in large measure, on keen parental involvement and on the fact that parents possess unique relationships with their children that educators must capitalize on. Put another way, you realize that partnering with parents is critical to your success as an educator.

As a school-community leader, you also are sensitive to that special relationship that exists between child and family. By reaching out to parents in such a way that solidifies that connection, you also strengthen your work with students in school. One school, for example, brings students and their families together once a month for about an hour and a half to "learn together." Parents may select from among a variety of workshops. Teachers, who volunteer for the sessions, may set out science projects or math games for families to explore. Or, they may show what students have learned over the course of a unit of instruction and may even celebrate with parents by planning and conducting a culminating activity of sorts. One school I have worked with sets aside time for parent and child to discuss a book or movie they have both seen. Teachers facilitate deep conversations about the book or movie. One parent commented, "This is the first time in a long time my son and I had a meaningful conversation centered on mutual learning." The students themselves may form a committee to plan a project or performance for the big event. Each family brings a packaged snack to share.

> "Schools need to remember that commitment, respect, time, and persistence on the part of educators result in lasting partnerships."
>
> —Concha Delgado Gaitan

The focus at the start of the hour is the learning experience, but as the kids inevitably become engrossed in learning together, their parents begin to visit with one another. By the end of the evening, a genuine sense of community has developed. Parents are encouraged to bring along other family members including spouses, children, and grandparents.

Such events may occur in the evening, where attendance is best, or before school, at lunchtime, or at other mutually convenient times. These "learn together" sessions generate much parent enthusiasm, support, and understanding. Parents get a chance to see how teachers teach various concepts. Teachers have an opportunity to meet with parents in a relaxed atmosphere of mutual learning. Teachers can gain much from observing families interact. Family photo opportunities are frequent. These photos are later displayed on school bulletin boards.

Reflective Questions

1. Can such an effort to learn together work in your school? Explain why or why not. If not, what can you do as school-community leaders to make this "best practice" a reality?

2. What alternate forms of "learning together" activities can be planned?

---

2. EMPOWER PARENTS

Parents have not always been welcomed partners in schools. At best, parents, historically, were viewed as important "educators" *at home* who were invaluable to support student learning, especially with respect to homework assistance. Their active involvement in schools, however, has only been a recent phenomenon. One of the most recent studies on parental involvement was undertaken by Sara Lawrence-Lightfoot (2003) who states, "If parents and teachers share close observations of children at home and school, these conversations have the potential to create holistic views of individual students and better address their learning needs" (p. 3). She conducted extensive observations across the country to better understand the nature of parent-teacher encounters. Parents, she maintains, often feel powerless. Parents from low socioeconomic groups and parents who are new immigrants are particularly vulnerable. Henderson and Mapp (2002) reaffirm this point by stating,

Furthermore, studies show that families of all income and education levels, and from all ethnic and cultural groups, are engaged in supporting their children's learning at home. White, middle-class families, however, tend to be more involved at school. Supporting more involvement at school from all families may be an important strategy for addressing the achievement gap. (p. 14)

Lawrence-Lightfoot continues by saying that these parents may appear withdrawn and apathetic, but in reality they feel dis-empowered. These parents need to be welcomed and provided assistance in order to navigate the intricacies of a school. Below are some strategies that might encourage parental empowerment:

- Hold more open school nights, albeit shorter in duration, in which information is conveyed to parents about the school.
- Provide parents who speak another language with transla-tors or translations of important school documents (e.g., letters to parents and other announcements).
- Ask parents to join in-school activities, committees, P.T.A., class mothers, and so on.
- Encourage parents to visit classrooms during various times of the year, not only during Open School week.
- Solicit parent volunteers to assist in various school activi-ties (e.g., lunchroom, before and after school).
- Ask parents to represent the school at various community functions (e.g., fairs, local civic meetings).
- Ask parents for feedback on a continual basis about opera-tions within the school.
- Go out of your way to greet and invite the participation of parents of groups usually disenfranchised or under-represented.

Reflective Question

1. In what other ways might you empower parents in your school? Provide specific examples and instances.

3. PROVIDE TRAINING

Scenario: At Stockton High School in an urban school district populated primarily of parents from low socioeconomic backgrounds, parents attend workshops in the evening as their children receive special tutoring by volunteer student teachers. Maria Rodriguez, a parent of two children in Grades 3 and 5, respectively, applauds the new program sponsored by the school and community. "I have a chance to take my G.E.D. course that leads to high school equivalency while my children receive help with their homework. I would never have had the opportunity to take these courses since I couldn't afford to pay for child care."

One of the more clever ideas for reaching out to parents was conveyed to me by my colleague, Lester Kostick, a former principal in New York City. At his school, parents, teachers, administrators, central office personnel, and volunteer community members plan a comprehensive training program for community parents. The following courses are offered between 6:00 p.m. and 10:00 p.m.:

- High school equivalency courses
- Pre-law
- Nutrition
- Early childhood care
- Child rearing
- English as a second language
- Street law (e.g., leases, immigration)
- Computers

At the same time, children attend special tutorial and enrichment classes offered by paid student teachers, overseen by a licensed teacher. Funding for the program may come from the district office, community fund-raising initiatives, special grants, and the like.

Reflective Questions

1. How might you implement Kostick's training program in your school?

2. What benefits might accrue from such an approach?

---

4. ESTABLISH PARENT COORDINATORS

In some school systems, such as that of New York City, each school has a paid parent coordinator who is hired expressly to generate interest among school and community parents. A major premise of the program is that reaching out to parents is best accomplished by another parent. Often, parents feel school officials are not approachable. A fellow parent may be more sensitive to their needs. These parent coordinators, selected by the school principal, organize weekly and monthly workshops in these areas, among others: literacy for adults and children, science fair help, English language learning, book making, homework assistance, time management skills, stress reduction, and so on. Parent coordinators plan and work very closely with the principal. These coordinators also serve to make further contacts within the community with social and health agencies and so forth.

Excerpts from an address by New York City School Chancellor Klein on the new position of Parent Coordinator, including other initiatives, and on parental involvement in general:

Catherine Man, May 25, 2004
http://www.insideschools.org/nv/
NV_help_wanted_may04.php

Parents, along with their children, of course, are the most important stakeholders in our public schools. If there is one thing that comes across loud and clear from parents in each and every Children First meeting, it's that we need to provide parents with multiple opportunities to communicate their views to decision-makers in our schools. Therefore, in order to more effectively engage parents and to ensure that we respond to their concerns at the local level, I will establish the position of Parent Coordinator in each school. The Parent Coordinator will be chosen by the principal and trained to play a key role in listening and responding to parent concerns. This significant addition of trained staff in the schools will serve as the first point of entry for parents to become more involved in their children's education. It is also the most significant point of contact for parents. Parents are primarily interested in what is going on in their children's school. As I have frequently said, and as we all know from our own experiences, parents send their children to a school, not to a school district or a school system.

But there are also times when issues are not, or cannot be, worked out at the school level. So, we are including a Parent Support Office in each of the ten Learning Support Centers that we will be establishing across the City. Each Support Office will be staffed by several Parent Support Officers—full-time staff who will supplement the engagement and response functions that our school-based Parent Coordinators will perform. Let me be clear: parents can go to any of these ten Offices, not just the one closest to their children's school. And, in order to make them as accessible to parents as possible, these Offices will be open two evenings a week and on weekends, in addition to regular business hours.

In addition, to bring greater clarity and coherence to the ways in which we engage parents in our schools and to offer parents concrete ways to learn more about what is going on with respect to the education of their children, we will create a Parent Academy. Through this Academy, Parent Coordinators will provide school-based workshops to parents on everything from understanding curriculum to forging the school-home connection and strengthening parent leadership and participation, including in key organizations like the Parent Associations and School Leadership Teams. Akin to the Leadership Academy for principals that was announced in December, the Parent Academy will be a full-service resource center with support and training for Parent Coordinators at the schools and Parent Support Officers at the Learning Support Centers.

This reference to our Leadership Academy provides a good transition to another key issue for parents. In the past days and weeks I have made clear that developing school leadership is a centerpiece of my Children First initiative. A great school leader understands that parents are key partners in the education of their children—both in terms of their involvement in their children's education and in terms of their responsibilities to their children. Parents must ensure that their children are education-focused and education-ready, that they get to school on time, that they behave in school, and that they do their homework. To that end, we will hold principals and schools accountable for ensuring parents do indeed feel like they are true partners. Parent engagement standards will be a part of each principal's performance review. Criteria will include the effectiveness of each school in successfully engaging parents, keeping them informed and addressing their concerns. For example, as

Mayor Bloomberg emphasized yesterday, principals will be expected to demonstrate a parent-welcoming school culture. This will include a set of clear expectations for all staff on showing consistent courtesy, responsiveness, sensitivity and respect towards parents. And parents will be given a meaningful opportunity to provide input into the evaluation of principal performance.

Against this backdrop, let me now turn to the historic school governance reform legislation, passed last June, which included a provision for community school boards to be eliminated by June 30, 2003, and which also established this Task Force and charged it with proposing a replacement to the Legislature. I want first to commend the Task Force for its fine work and emphasize that we look forward to working with you in devising and effectively implementing your important proposal. In that regard, the replacement for community school boards that we are outlining today— Parent Engagement Boards—would play an important role in shaping various aspects of the educational debate, including budget, educational policy and zoning. In fact, this proposal will provide more parents with better and more entry points and a stronger voice on behalf of their children's education.

These Parent Engagement Boards should be made up of parents selected from the different schools within their district. And, in our view, they should have several functions in common with the current community school boards, as well as some new ones. Members of Parent Engagement Boards will meet regularly with the Regional Superintendents, who will be responsible for instructional oversight of the schools in their districts, to review their schools' progress. In addition, these Parent Engagement Boards should have input into the evaluation of Regional Superintendents and their Local Instructional Supervisors. This is a critical means of building a system that is responsive to parents by having them play an important role in evaluating key instructional personnel.

Furthermore, I would like the Boards to be another avenue for parents with concerns. In effect, the Boards would have an ombudsperson function. I know that this is an important aspect of the current community school boards, and the Parent Engagement Boards should be of even greater assistance to the parents in that they will all be parents themselves. Indeed, they should monitor and advise as to how our parent initiatives at the schools and in the Parent Support Offices are working.

Reflective Questions

1. How might this innovation in New York City be adopted in your school or district?

2. What is your reaction to this position of parent coordinator that operates independent of parent P.T.A. volunteers?

---

5. FOSTER PARENTAL SUCCESS

Thompson's (2005) eight steps to parental success offer insights to principals who believe in the value of parental participation. Parents and teachers should work in consonance with each other to ensure that the student's educational needs are met. Teachers and parents should collaborate through discussions and in-person meetings to reach agreement about a child's strengths and challenges and to unite on the best ways they each can respond to them. Thompson, the author of *The Pressured Child: Helping Your Child to Achieve Success in School,* outlines eight steps that parents should take to help their children. Principals can do much to reinforce such knowledge. As principal, you can offer workshops, for instance, to parents and teachers to share Thompson's suggestions:

1. Be there. Thompson recommends that both parents should attend parent-teacher conferences to demonstrate that they care about their child's progress. Often, parents will say, "Honey, why don't you go meet the teacher alone?" Thompson says, "Research shows that children do better academically when both parents attend conferences and PTA meetings" (p. 49). Parents should be encouraged to attend these conferences throughout a child's schooling experience, including middle and high school education.

2. Remember the F word: Focus. Focus conversations on positive ways to assist the student by developing practical, feasible strategies for school success. Parents should be encouraged to focus by asking teachers pertinent questions when they meet. For example, "How do you expect me to help my child with the science fair project?" Teachers should also be prepared to deal with varied questions parents might ask such as, "What's the school mission?"

"How can I get more involved?" "Can I join the school Leadership Team?" "Does my child need a tutor?" "What can we do at home to ensure that our child succeeds in school?" "Can my child have extra textbooks to study from?" "Why does my child complain that she's not called on enough in class?" Remember, focus your responses positively and constructively.

3. Share insider information. Teachers should establish a respectful, open atmosphere so that parents feel comfortable to share information about their child. Parents can convey to teachers invaluable information about how the child learns best or about what motivates the child that could prove useful to the classroom teacher. Also included here is information the teacher can convey to illustrate the student's behavior in class. A teacher I once knew actually tape recorded the child's outburst in class. When the parent denied that her child could ever act that way, the teacher played the tape for the parent. I don't suggest this strategy because of the ethical considerations at play here, not to mention how the parent might react to such measures. At best though, the teacher convincingly provided the parent with realistic "insider" information.

4. Use a report card as a jumping-off point, not as a centerpiece of discussion. "Teachers should get discussion beyond the particular grade to more detailed observations about what's working and what's not" (p. 49). Both parents and teachers need to be reminded to focus on how to best help the student learn. The grade is merely a means to start discussion.

5. Inquire about your child's progress in areas that aren't easily measured by grades. The student's social development is critically important. What are the positive or not-so-positive character traits displayed by the student? How might both the teacher and parent encourage better character traits such as treating others with respect, getting along with others, and going out of one's way to assist someone else?

6. Ask what you can do. Parents see the teacher as the educational expert, but they also will solicit advice from the teacher in regard to noneducational matters such as best ways to manage student behavior at home. Teachers should be counseled to offer some advice but to also refer the parent to specialists who might be better trained to assist them. Parents too should feel comfortable to ask the teacher how they might be able to reinforce desired

behaviors at home initiated by the classroom teacher. Such conversations between teacher and parent may result in better management of student behavior both at home and school. When parents and teacher partner in these ways, students receive consistent, not contradictory, messages.

7. Trust your child's development. Building trust between teacher and parent is critical to the development of the child. When parents and teachers work in unison, a mutual feeling of trust and confidence should ensue that the child is proceeding well, academically and socially. Further discussions between parent and teacher can result in modifications.

8. Leave your own school baggage at home. Avoid preconceived notions about each other. Prejudices run deep. Uncover any prejudgments a teacher might make about, for instance, the ethnic background of the parent or a prejudgment a parent might make with a teacher, based perhaps on a previous experience with last year's teacher. Enter the dialogue with the notion that both teacher and parent are there to work together to guide the student to success.

As principal, it is critically important to train new teachers how to run a conference. Providing staff development is suggested. Perhaps even encourage more experienced teachers to buddy with new teachers to offer advice and mentoring. Doing so will not only benefit the new teachers but also empower the more experienced teaching professionals.

Reflective Questions

1. How might you utilize Thompson's suggestions in your work with teachers and parents?

2. What would you as principal add?

---

6. PUBLICIZE STUDENT PRESENTATIONS

Fiore (2002) suggests that the very act of presenting students to the school goes a long way toward strengthening parent-school ties. He explains, "Unfortunately, many school leaders squander opportunities to involve members of their school's external publics in presentations and exhibitions by students" (p. 113). He goes to explain that involving the public in such activities can "show a great deal about a school's strengths, while increasing the number of people attending in support of children" (p. 113). Invite the external public to the following student in-school presentations:

- Athletic events
- School plays (e.g., musicals, dramas)
- Artistic events (including artwork, musical recitals)
- Academic competitions (including spelling bees, science fairs)
- Open house tours (e.g., classroom visits)
- Ordinary in-class student presentations
- Convocations and celebrations (e.g., award programs)

Of course, anyone you invite should be a known community member, as we must always be wary of safety and security issues.

Fiore suggests that parents welcome opportunities to see their children perform or showcase their work. Fiore recommends that principals develop an agenda or plan to involve parents prior to the event or presentation. In other words, have specific tasks you want particular parents to be involved in. Solicit their participation at the event. He also advocates extensive use of newsletters as follow-ups to such events. He states that "a great deal of written communication is essential in all successful school-community relations plans" (p. 141). He also recommends judicious use of e-mail, Web pages, and personal letters from the principal to enhance parental support and involvement.

Reflective Question

1. How might you utilize Fiore's suggestions in your work with parents?

---

7. SOLICIT PARENT AND COMMUNITY INVOLVEMENT

In reviewing extant literature on school effectiveness in terms of promoting student achievement, Marzano (2003) highlights the importance of parental and community involvement. Not all parental and community involvement yields positive effects on schools. Clearly, if parents merely criticize school officials without substantive involvement to create new and better ways of doing things, such participation can even serve to erode relationships and create a negative atmosphere in a school. Marzano addresses three features that define effective parental and community involvement: communication, participation, and governance.

• Communication—Good communication, initiated by the principal, is key. Good principals use all of the following ways to communicate to parents: newsletters, bulletins, and flyers. As in any human relationship, communication is critical for building and sustaining alliances with the community.

• Participation—Physical participation is critical. Community members may serve as teacher aides, guest lecturers, and tutors. Such participation may result in extended expertise in various content areas, additional external resources for the school, direct financial contributions, and donations from businesses (Tangri & Moles, 1987, as cited by Marzano, 2003). Marzano explains that participation in the everyday functioning of the school results in "reported lower absenteeism, truancy, and dropout rates" (p. 48).

• Governance—Giving voice to community members is essential to build and sustain alliances between school and community. Marzano relates that research indicates that community members are less interested in being involved in hiring and firing of school personnel than in "decisions regarding programs and practices that bore directly on the achievement of their children" (p. 49).

Marzano goes on to identify three action steps that best promote parent and community involvement:

• Establish vehicles for communication between schools and parents and the community. The following specific activities are recommended: (a) Issue all communiqués (including public meetings) in languages relevant to student populations in the school. (b) Make information about the school readily available and easily attainable. (c) Maintain ongoing communications via e-mail, Web pages, home visits, and parent-teacher conferences. Research demonstrates that principals' direct involvement in sustaining effective communication is very important to building alliances.

• Establish multiple ways for parents and community to be involved in the day-to-day running of the school. Research shows that when the community develops a sense of ownership, positive effects are common. Marzano highlights the use of volunteers as most critical. Principals who solicit the involvement of volunteers also provide orientation workshops and ongoing training for them.

• Establish governance vehicles that allow for the involvement of parents and community members. Marzano highlights the famous Comer model of community involvement that involves three "mechanisms": (a) School Planning and Management Team—comprising teachers, parents, professional specialists, community volunteers, and nonprofessional staff. The purpose of the team is to establish curriculum policies related to "overall school environment and staff development" (p. 51); implement, coordinate, and evaluate school activities; and work with the community to "establish a calendar for social and informational activities" (p. 51). (b) Student and Staff Support Team—Although this aspect does not include community membership, the team gives feedback to the previous team on the effectiveness of the curricular programming in the school. (c) Parent Team—an all-parent team that gives parents a variety of options for participating in school governance. Marzano mentions other forms of governance that are also research based.

Reflective Question

1. To what extent are the aforementioned ways of building community alliances feasible in your school? Explain in detail.

---

8. DEVELOP PARENT INVOLVEMENT ACTIVITIES

Young (2004) summarizes the research on parental involvement succinctly: "Students do better in school when their parents are involved" (p. 112). Proactive school-community leaders find ways of involving parents. Although parents are busy and the challenge is enormous, your approach to parental involvement is key. Maintain an optimistic, inviting demeanor and select several of these "ideas that can enhance parent involvement" (quoted from Young, pp. 112–113):

- Parent luncheons
- Classroom visitations
- Father-son, mother-daughter breakfasts
- Grandparent days
- Phone calls home with positive messages (goes a long way toward building trust and good will)
- Videos and recordings of newsletters for parents who can't read or see
- Curriculum nights
- Parent workshops
- New parents night
- School tours
- Formal invitations to assemblies
- Read-ins
- Career-sharing days
- Clean-up days

Reflective Questions

1. How might you incorporate the activities above?

2. What other suggestions can you offer to involve parents?

CONCLUSION

School-community leaders use a variety of means of involving parents. This chapter has highlighted only a few. Principals will complain from time to time that parents are reluctant to participate in schools. Proactive school-community leaders who deeply believe that parental involvement is critical to student achievement (Henderson & Berla, 1994) will remain optimistic and

> *"Schools cannot do it alone— cannot be all things to all students. . . . The community school approach makes it possible for teachers, administrators, parents, and community partners to work together and support each other as a strong coalition."*
>
> —Gerald Tirozzi

committed in their quest to meaningfully and continually involve parents.

Parental involvement, however, remains only a part of an overall plan of the school-community principal leader. Connecting to others in the community who might positively affect student learning is equally important. Forging meaningful, appropriate community alliances that go beyond parental involvement is also essential to school-community leadership, a subject that the next chapter will address.

C H A P T E R   T H R E E

Best Practices in Building Community Alliances

"School-community partnerships . . . can be defined as the connections between schools and community individuals, organizations, and businesses that are forged to promote students' social, emotional, physical, and intellectual development."

—Mavis G. Sanders

"A community-empowered school is one in which all members of the community—administrators, teachers, school staff, students, parents, and members of the local community at large—participate in efforts to achieve a school's goal of improving student performance."

—Mary Ann Burke and Lawrence O. Picus

In discussing a constructivist approach to community, Arriaza (2004) frames community as "a source of knowledge that educators need to access in order to understand the cultural, social, and linguistic barriers that separate schools from the communities they serve" (p. 14). Constructivists, according to Arriaza, "consider a community the school's natural extension since its students exhibit cultural traits that spring from within the community they come from. In this sense," he continues, "educators strongly encourage the school's involvement in the community's social events as long as this implement yields knowledge" (pp. 14–15). This way of thinking obligates communities to commit to assisting schools by giving "resources (tangible and intangible) and services needed" (p. 15).

How Can Schools, Families, and Community Groups Put These Findings into Action?

- Recognize that all parents, regardless of income, education, or cultural background, are involved in their children's learning and want their children to do well.
- Design programs that will support families to guide their children's learning, from preschool through high school.
- Develop the capacity of school staff and families to work together.
- Link efforts to engage families, whether based at school or in the community, in student learning.
- Build families' social and political connections.
- Embrace a philosophy of partnership and be willing to share power. Focus on developing trusting and respectful relationships. Make sure that parents, school staff, and community members understand that the responsibility for children's educational development is a collaborative enterprise.
- Build strong connections between schools and community organizations.
- Include families in all strategies to reduce the achievement gap between white, middle-class students and low-income students and students of color.

SOURCE: From *A New Generation of Evidence: The Family Is Critical to Student Achievement*, by Anne T. Henderson and Nancy Berla (Washington, DC: Center for Law and Education, 1994) and *A New Wave of Evidence: The Impact of School, Family and Community Connections on Student Achievement*, by Anne T. Henderson and Karen L. Mapp (Austin, TX: Southwest Educational Development Laboratory, 2002). Retrieved from http://www.ncpie.org/pubs/NewWaveofEvidenceJan2003.doc

This chapter will highlight varied ways you as the principal can apply some or all of these constructivist approaches to community.

**What You Should Know
About Building Community Alliances**

- **Consider Six Types of Involvement**—Epstein et al.'s six types of community involvement form the foundation of any community alliance.
- **Form Community Advisory Committees**—Community advisory boards are practical ways of involving a relatively large number of community constituents.
- **Undertake Community Building**—Reynolds offers several practical tips for building community support.
- **Plan Together**—Gretz's planning phases for establishing school-community relations are discussed.
- **Develop an After-School Program**—Principals should get involved in developing after-school curricula matched to during-the-day school curricula, as well as familiarizing themselves with successful after-school programs that have a community focus (Fashola's work).
- **Involve Parents and Community**—Young's tips for engaging the community are highlighted.
- **Avoid Barriers to Implementation**—Cushing and Cole's three barriers to implementing a community initiative are addressed as well as Sanders's strategies for overcoming them.
- **Become Media Savvy**—Ubben, Hughes, and Norris's suggestions for dealing with the media are reviewed.
- **Become Part of a Professional Development School (PDS) Initiative**—Collaborating with a local college or university is a unique opportunity to forge a community alliance that can pay dividends for student achievement.

---

1. CONSIDER SIX TYPES OF INVOLVEMENT

I don't think that any principal would say that community involvement isn't necessary. Yet few principals go out of their way to articulate and organize a well-planned community partnership program. Research demonstrates clearly that well-organized partnership programs linked to school strategic plans are successful (Epstein & Salinas, 2004). Principals who plan and organize community involvement consider six frames or approaches (Epstein et al., 2002):

- Parenting—Clearly, community involvement begins with the parent and the family structure. Principals can help community involvement by assisting families with parenting skills. Effective principals recognize parents and families as the first and enduring educators. Yet, parents need training to educate effectively. Principals help by providing families with an understanding of child and adolescent development as well as strategies of positive or cooperative discipline that promote and reinforce the work of teachers in the classroom. Workshops can be provided to families on learning how to establish a warm, supportive physical and emotional home environment for learning. Epstein et al. also state that parenting includes assisting schools in understanding families' backgrounds, cultures, and goals for children.

- Communicating—Principals play a critical role in this type of involvement. Communication goes far beyond simply sending letters home, even on a regular and consistent basis. Communication more importantly involves opening channels so that parents can effectively reach and contact school officials. Two-way communication with families may involve information about special school programs, school services for students and families, and reports of student progress.

- Volunteering—Principals can contribute greatly by soliciting community volunteers with varying degrees of expertise to work in the school. Special tutors, person-power to assist with lunch duty responsibilities, and individuals to help with office work may be useful.

- Learning at Home—Principals who get parents involved with their children's work at home influence student achievement positively. Workshops on assisting children with homework and projects are useful. These workshops should be repeated often to involve as many families as possible.

- Decision Making—Family involvement is more than involving parents in mundane activities. Serious commitment to community involvement that builds lasting alliances involves inviting families as participants in school governance, school leadership teams, advocacy groups, and other relevant committees.

- Collaborating with Community—Principals actualize their roles as school-community leaders when they involve businesses, agencies, cultural and civic organizations, and colleges and universities.

Epstein and Salinas (2004) explain,

By implementing activities for all six types of involvement, schools can help parents become involved at school and at home in various ways that meet student needs and family schedules. Input from participants helps schools address challenges and improve plans, activities, and outreach so that all families can be productive partners in their children's school success. (p. 13)

The authors highlight several efforts by various schools nationwide aimed at addressing these types of involvement:

- Evening discussions at a middle school to help parents learn about effective parenting strategies for their adolescents that reinforce in-school strategies
- Weekly newsletters that highlight one instructional strategy parents can use at home
- Afternoon and evening literacy circles where parents discuss books and other forms of literature
- Father-son and mother-daughter breakfasts
- The Second Cup of Coffee Program

- Story telling (e.g., humor, scary) among parents, senior citizens, and community groups; students judge the best stories and tell their own as well
- Reading-at-home workshops
- Spanish books distribution program
- Family album sharing
- Take-home bag of math or science materials
- Career nights
- College preparation program
- Local martial arts instructors invited to demonstrate and teach self-defense
- Bag-a-lunch program
- Pen pals with senior citizens
- Dinner to honor students and teachers who reach out to the community
- Fund-raising in community to support field trips to museums and other educational settings
- Two-way community service—While families are provided health information on a wide variety of topics at a community health fair, students reciprocate by engaging in community service by visiting hospital patients and/or displaying artwork in hospital corridors

---

Reflective Question

1. To what extent are the aforementioned ideas feasible in your school? Explain in detail.

---

2. FORM A COMMUNITY ADVISORY COMMITTEE

As school-community leader, you realize that a school-community based program needs guidance and support. The literature on such efforts indicates that forming a community advisory board, made up of stakeholders from both the school and community (e.g., owners of businesses, presidents of clubs or associations, chairs and deans at colleges), is important for efficient and effective program operation (Fashola, 2002). These advisory boards either serve as advisors to the school principal or superintendent or serve in their capacity as policy or decision makers.

Community advisory boards strengthen the bonds between school and community. Partners work closely together over extended periods of time addressing common problems and issues. An advisory board formalizes ongoing collaborations and community-based activities. As communities become increasingly complex, such boards help navigate community politics by bringing together key constituents to problem-solve seemingly intractable issues. Community advisory committees also serve as a buffer to thwart external influences from pressure groups, which might not have

> *"Communities are organized around relationships and the felt interdependencies that nurture them."*
>
> —Thomas J. Sergiovanni

the best interests of your school in mind (e.g., commercial enterprises who want to use your school to sell their product wherein profit, not student academic success, is the bottom line).

Community advisory groups also interact with more formal structures including local school boards, boards of education, state education agencies, and even the federal government, as relevant and needed (for a good discussion of such committees, see Ubben, Hughes, & Norris, 2004).

Reflective Question

1. To what extent are community advisory boards feasible in your school? Explain in detail.

---

3. UNDERTAKE COMMUNITY BUILDING

It's not easy to convince the community to join the school in partnerships. Many of you might know principals who will attest to this fact. Perhaps you have come up short in your experience. Sure, you'll find the irate parent who continually complains or the businessperson who has a vested interest in marketing his product in your school who will get involved. But to encourage community members who truly believe in contributing positively to student growth is not so simple. So how do you attract those kinds of individuals or groups? How do you build community support for your school? Reynolds (2002) offers several practical tips for building community support.

Reynolds suggests that it is indeed difficult and rare to attract the true altruist, nor should you really try to. Your efforts, he explains, should be to "make the events that take place at the school mutually beneficial to both the school and the community" (p. 81). Here are a few of his suggestions:

• Community Night—Teachers and student delegates from the Future Teacher's program teach evening classes to members of the community.

• Community2000 Lock-In—Reynolds explains, "Our Community2000 group (sponsored by a teacher in our district, local police officers, and community members) volunteer an evening to supervise middle level and high school students who want to spend a night in our school playing games and having fun. Local patrons donate prizes for the students to win" (p. 81).

• Community Betterment Project—Students at the school volunteer after school and weekends to "help with various landscaping projects for businesses" in the community.

• Food Pantry Distribution—Reynolds explains, "Members of our student body volunteer time to help unload trucks at a local church to ensure that our community food pantry is well-stocked when people in our community are in need" (p. 82).

• Share Resources—Schools partner with local chapters of national associations, other schools, and area organizations to promote community goodwill by engaging in the following activities (p. 82):

* Staff members and the local police force produce a DARE graduation program for elementary school students as part of a drug-free program.

* A neighboring school uses another school's gymnasium and multipurpose buildings for athletic contests.

* The Future Business Leaders of America organization sponsors a blood drive in the gymnasium for the community.

* The Family, Career and Community Leaders of America organization collects Toys for Tots for families within the community.

Reflective Questions

1. What is the benefit to both school and community for each of Reynolds's suggestions? For example, for Community Night, Reynolds states the benefits as follows: "Our students benefit by teaching a skill they have mastered, and our community benefits by learning new skills—for example, how to use a digital camera or how to create a webpage" (p. 82).

2. Which of Reynolds's suggestions might work in your school? Explain.

3. How would you convince a community member without children to partner somehow with your school?

---

4. PLAN TOGETHER

According to Gretz (2003), "Planning is the most important ingredient to establishing a successful partnership" (p. 32). By planning school-community projects of mutual benefit, strong community alliances are formed. Gretz identifies several key ingredients or phases of the planning process:

• Establish goals. Gretz states, "The goals should be general statements that express specific desired outcomes and are based on needs, reflect available resources, and are easily understood by all members of the partnership" (p. 33).

• Assess needs. Gretz writes, "Although there are broad areas of need that are universally true to all school-community partnerships, each principal must assess the specific needs that are unique to his or her school. All businesses seek skilled employees, but what particular skills do the businesses that are involved look for? Can certain skill areas be identified and incorporated into the goals? How can the business contribute to the school curriculum? These types of questions help guide the planning phase and ensure that the community is truly engaged" (pp. 33–34).

- Develop vision. Gretz states, "The vision must express the values of the group. Although a vision statement expresses the dream, the goals are the practical ambitions of the stakeholders and should be tied to measurable outcomes" (p. 33).

- Decide management issues. Gretz explains, "Managing a partnership in which students, parents, business leaders, and community members are involved requires a delicate balance of delegation and control that enables stakeholders to participate and share responsibility and yet clearly define and understand the different roles that are involved in a successful partnership" (p. 34).

"Neglecting any of these elements can significantly impair the partnership's ability to influence what actually happens in the school" (p. 33).

Planning inevitably entails assessment. How do you know this plan has been actualized and is meeting its stated goals? Gretz identifies three approaches that have "proven to be both innovative and effective":

Portfolios. Comprehensive collections of data that represent the progress and accomplishments of the partnership can be compiled in a scrapbook and displayed for visitors or published on the Internet. This can serve as an effective recruitment tool for potential future partners or funders.

Murals. Students can create wall paintings to express the concepts represented within the partnership.

Surveys. Members of the partnering groups and school community can complete surveys that assess satisfaction and perception. (p. 35)

Gretz ends his brief yet insightful article by quoting Lyndon Johnson:

"The best time to make friends is before you need them." As school leaders facing the challenges of recreating the idea of how schools can best support student achievement, we need to have friends within the community who will encourage our efforts and supplement our programs. Now is undoubtedly the best time for us to cultivate these relationships and get our communities involved. (p. 35)

Reflective Question

1. How might you incorporate Gretz's ideas for building community alliances?

---

5. DEVELOP AN AFTER-SCHOOL PROGRAM

Developing an after-school program matched to what you do during the school day is important. Although many schools offer after-school programs, very few of these programs have developed a curriculum and learning activities that offer either enrichment or remediation to students who attend school during the day. The best after-school programs are intentionally planned to support learning that takes place during the school day in school.

Successful school-community leaders, then, take an active role in shaping and influencing curricula in after-school programs (see Chapter 4 for further discussion of this point). Here are a few suggestions for getting started:

- Conduct a needs assessment. What after-school program already exists? Was there one in the past? What happened to it? Who controls the programming (private enterprise, school district, or the school itself)? What authority might you have to get involved in shaping the curriculum of the after-school program? Who are the students attending the after-school program? What are their educational needs?

- Solicit approval for helping to coordinate the after-school curriculum. Serve as an advocate for the after-school program.

Demonstrate why involvement in the after-school program benefits your students academically.

- Form a curriculum committee. Involve teachers, parents, and professional specialists to help review after-school curricula and offer suggestions for better matching after-school learning activities with in-school activities.

- Train teachers. Offer professional development opportunities for teachers who work in the after-school program. Assist them, particularly, in providing appropriate remediation and/or enrichment lessons matched to the special needs of each student who attends that school.

After-school programs may have different purposes and foci, not always primarily academic. Still, these efforts build strong community alliances that can, at the very least, indirectly affect achievement. Often we learn best not from what others describe as best practice, but from what we see in action. Fashola (2002) describes several successful after-school programs that have a community focus. You can learn best from them, however, if you have an opportunity to visit and observe a program in action; doing so will indeed strengthen your commitment to building community alliances. Below are three such successful programs culled from Fashola (2002):

- New York City Beacons

Approximately 40 New York City schools currently have beacon programs. "The main goal of the program is to reduce crime and violence among youth and their families by providing after-school programs for the whole family, to ultimately improve school and community linkages" (p. 45). Educational, cultural, and recreational activities, workshops and programs are available for the whole family. Family services are provided to support family in the areas of social welfare, language acquisition skills, family counseling, and health-related services. Fashola describes four main goals of the program as follows:

The Beacons have four main goals: youth development, parental involvement and family support, school-home-community linkages, and building safe and supportive neighborhoods for child and youth development.

The youth development aspect of the program aims to provide students with a sense of community. Youth are engaged in challenging and engaging activities that allow them to participate meaningfully in decision making, with a goal of eliminating such challenges to teenagers as violence, substance abuse, juvenile delinquency, and teenage pregnancy.

The improved school-home-community linkages strive to use the school as an educational forum that changes and forms the community into a goal oriented network of youth and adults, school staff members, schools as a whole, and minority communities. Some of the goals of these linkages include increasing school attendance and improving community problem-solving capabilities. The schools and Department of Youth and Community Development also collaborate with the Administration for Children's Services to provide additional social services for the children involved in the Beacons program.

Parental involvement in the Beacons program includes getting parents to help in the after-school program and offering opportunities for the adults to improve themselves through adult education, cultural, and recreation classes during the non-school hours. As they strive to improve relations between schools and parents, the Beacons staff members help parents by accompanying them to meetings with school staff and by hosting parent-teacher Beacons meetings. (p. 46)

- Child First Authority (CFA)

The Child First Authority is a Baltimore community-based after-school program that seeks to improve the quality of life in low socioeconomic-status communities. The CFA received funding from the mayor's office, the governor, and the city council through a local Industrial Areas Foundation branch named Baltimoreans United in Leadership Development (BUILD) in the summer of 1996. During the first year of funding, the CFA established community-based learning centers in 10 schools. The main goal of this program is to improve the quality of life in Baltimore City by directly serving public school students and their families academically, culturally, and behaviorally in the school-based, extended-day centers. The program used the schools as hubs of activity in which parents, staff members, administrators, church members, students, and other community members get together. Although the overall goal of the program is the improvement of the quality of life, the CFA programs in the schools in Baltimore are not all the same. BUILD oversees the program as a whole and specifies the parent and community components of the program, but the programs have evolved differently from site to site. For example, different extended-school-day centers have chosen to use different cultural enrichment programs, depending on the needs and the goals of the program planning teams. (p. 49)

- Big Brothers Big Sisters of America

Big Brothers Big Sisters of America was created specifically to provide young children from single-parent families with adult mentors. The organization is mainly funded by the U.S. Department of Justice. The goal of this program is to provide young children (especially inner-city children and children from single-parent homes) with role models in their everyday lives who will provide them with positive experiences, teach them to make healthy decisions, and help them strive for the best in life.

Children participate in Big Brothers Big Sisters by connecting with local agencies, but there is a waiting list. Adults who sign up to be Big Brothers and Big Sisters are screened and, if selected, asked to spend at least 4 to 6 hours every month with their little brothers or sisters. (p. 50)

Reflective Question

1. How might these aforementioned ideas about after-school programs assist you in building stronger community alliances?

---

6. INVOLVE PARENTS AND COMMUNITY

Young (2004) presents a number of easy-to-implement strategies for involving parents and engaging in community alliances that you, as principal, might find useful.

- Engage the community. As principal you "must have vision and take the lead in making things . . . happen" (p. 107). Young suggests a very creative way to do so that he culled from the Ohio Association of Elementary School Administrators. SWAP, "Supervision with a Principal," is a program in which the principal invites "a guest from the community to shadow" him for a day. "In return," explains Young, "the principal swaps and learns the work world of the invited guest" (p. 106). At a public forum later in the year, the two individuals discuss their experiences and insights into one another's position. A strong bond develops between the two individuals. The school benefits because the community member better understands the needs of the school and perhaps the businessperson may be more apt to, for instance, donate funds to the school to support some aspect of the educational program.

- Be the cheerleader for your school. Young encourages principals to speak often about why the school's mission is so important. He says, "Many principals do not like to 'toot their own horns.' If you don't, few others will" (p. 108). Proactive school-community leaders do not shy away from their responsibility to "sell" their school. Your enthusiasm for your school will catch on and spread throughout the community.

- Maintain a current Web site for the school. Young states, "Having a school Web site is a great way to advertise your school's accomplishments" (p. 110). Web pages can herald your school and solicit community involvement very differently than can personal contacts. Although the personal touch is essential, principals who do not use the Internet as an out-reach tool are missing an invaluable opportunity to make special connections. If you can include a video clip of your school on your page, you will be able to highlight special features or programs in your school. Many parents and community members may not have the time to actually spend much time in your school, but they can stay attuned and feel part of the school community at work or at home by accessing a Web page that is as warm and inviting as it is informational.

- Listen. This seemingly simplistic advice is perhaps one of the best ways to engender good will and community involvement.

Whenever anyone enters your office, stop what you are doing. Look up, smile, and give them your full attention. Paraphrase what they have said to demonstrate that you have in fact listened.

As we end this best practice of involving parents, it should be noted that we as principals should proactively reach out to all parents in a given community. It is not uncommon for principals to overlook, albeit unintentionally, marginalized parents (e.g., non-English-speaking parents, parents with disabilities). We can do much here to involve such marginalized groups. Here are a few suggestions:

- Personally invite them to school functions.
- Offer any reasonable, special assistance they may need to attend.
- Provide translations of school memoranda in relevant languages.
- Provide translators at various functions.
- Hire sign language communicators.
- Bring in guest speakers on topics of interest to these parents.
- Always be available to meet with them.
- Don't wait for them to approach you; remain proactive.

Reflective Question

1. How useful are the aforementioned tips for involving parents and community? Describe more precisely how they can build stronger community alliances.

---

7. AVOID BARRIERS TO IMPLEMENTATION

Principals, like yourself, who are committed to school-community leadership inevitably encounter obstacles to implementing school-community collaborations. Remaining aware of these obstacles is critical to success. Proactive, not reactive, school-community leaders take affirmative steps to build and sustain community alliances. Cushing and Cole (1997, as cited by Sanders, 2001) identify three barriers to successful collaborations.

- Fear of public scrutiny. One of the greatest and most prescient fears administrators have is attracting negative media coverage. They realize publicity can cut both ways. At times, it's difficult to anticipate how the media might respond. Even though a principal might have good relationships with a reporter, for instance, she might not write a favorable story about a questionable episode that has occurred in the school.

- Staff burnout. As principal, you might build many community bridges and overcommit your staff to extra work, which is inevitable in collaborations. Teachers, for instance, might be exhausted or stressed by excessive demands on their time above and beyond their in-school responsibilities.

- Negative attitudes about the community. Some educators might harbor prejudices or simply negative attitudes about a community's ability or willingness to collaborate. Some teachers, for instance, might label parents of students from low socioeconomic backgrounds as uncaring about the education of their children.

Building on these obstacles and identifying others, Sanders (2001) conducted an in-depth study exploring, in part, the challenges schools face in developing community partnerships as well as strategies to address these obstacles to community alliances. Sanders's insights are instructive for our work as principal school-community leaders. The first challenge Sanders identifies is that of "participation," more precisely "insufficient participation" (p. 26). This challenge can cut both ways as is illustrated in these two scenarios:

1. Principal: "Our school-community initiative got off to a real slow start because we couldn't identify enough community volunteers (i.e., parents and local business people) who were willing to commit long-term."

2. Principal: "Our school-community initiative got off to a real slow start because we couldn't identify enough teachers and school staff members willing to participate in the after-school program."

Sanders presents several strategies for overcoming the barrier of "insufficient participation":

Some suggested reaching out beyond faculty members to volunteer for help in coordinating partnership activities. Some suggested using local media and school newsletters to increase awareness of activities. Still others mentioned making reminder phone calls encouraging participants to bring friends to activities, and providing door prizes and other incentives for participation. Other strategies included changing the time of activities to accommodate more interested individuals; organizing Saturday as well as weekday functions; providing transportation, food, and baby-sitting services; and using community facilities for activities. (p. 27)

A second, related barrier that Sanders identifies is that of "insufficient time" (p. 27). Finding the time to meet and implement community partnerships can be a major difficulty. Sanders suggests successful strategies for overcoming this barrier.

They suggested that schools identify a wider range of staff and parent and community volunteers to plan and implement activities. They . . . could organize into committees responsible for specific tasks so that frequent meetings . . . are not required. Some respondents suggested that schools hire facilitators to help . . . coordinate partnership activities; others mentioned that . . . [they] could plan activities in the spring or summer of each school year so that they are ready to implement activities in the fall, . . . hold meetings before or after school or use volunteers to cover classrooms so that teachers have time to meet during the school day. (p. 27)

A third obstacle to building and sustaining community alliances involves the community itself, or at least the perceptions others have about the community. "Resource-poor communities" (p. 27) are problematic in that they have few businesses or other community-based organizations. Sanders also cites competition among schools; scarce community resources cause stress and represent a key barrier to implementation. To address these barriers, Sanders suggests that schools expand their database of potential community partners. Principals might solicit interest among universities and colleges, health care organizations, government agencies, volunteer organizations, faith organizations, senior citizen groups, and/or agencies outside their geographic neighborhood. Sanders and Harvey (2002) provide a more detailed array of possible collaborations with the community:

1. *A nonprofit health organization.* The organization is affiliated with a school of medicine in the city. The organization was created to assist in the prevention of hypertension and diabetes in high-risk communities. . . . The organization also worked with the school to survey families about their knowledge of health care issues. In addition, the organization sponsored a good nutrition poster competition and a healthy cooking competition for students and their parents.

2. *A collaboration between a community-based initiative and a local church.* The collaborating organizations implement an after school program with academic, cultural, and behavioral objectives for students. Students are assisted with homework, attend field trips, and engage in recreational and cultural activities. The program begins at 2:30 p.m. and ends at 5:15 p.m., Monday through Friday. The after-school program has a predesigned parent/community involvement component, which includes a 4-hour per month volunteer requirement. Parents can volunteer or have representatives, such as older siblings, grandparents, and other family members, volunteer for them. The program is offered free of cost to its participants.

3. *A health care facility.* The facility provides health information to staff, students, and parents through workshops and classroom presentations. Topics have included cholesterol management, HIV prevention and treatment, Attention Deficit Disorder, parenting skills, diabetes management, and CPR certification. The organization also provides refreshments for, and volunteers to help implement, school events, such as family fun and learning nights, father and son banquets, and the end-of-year picnic. The organization also sponsors a student academic recognition program, which honors academically successful students at quarterly awards breakfasts.

4. *A nonprofit foundation.* The foundation sponsors the hundred Book Challenge program. Participating schools are provided with rotating classroom libraries with books that are color coded by level. Teachers assess students' reading levels and assign them colors. Students select books coded with

these colors and read, in class, 30 minutes each day. Students also are encouraged to take books home and read to their parents. Every book that the child reads is recorded, and after a certain number are read children receive incentives, such as pens and pencils. Students who read 100 books or more are recognized at the school's quarterly awards breakfasts.

5. *A suburban elementary school.* The PTA at this elementary school has provided the case school with books for more than 2 years. The partner school also shared with the case school a book credit that allowed the school to purchase new books from Scholastic Press. The school formally adopted the case school during the 1999–2000 school year and hopes to expand their exchange and interaction.

6. *A health care company.* The company has a community outreach initiative, Partnership in Education program, that includes about 42 volunteers who work with three schools. Seven volunteers from this company support the case school in a variety of ways. They act as tutors for students with academic problems. They also hold book drives for the school. During the 1998–99 school year, the company donated 600 books to the school. The company also has donated several computers to the school that are used in the school's computer center.

7. *A local church.* The church has an outreach committee that provides school supplies to students in need, and also provides refreshments for school parties, including Valentine's Day and Christmas parties. Members of the outreach committee also have worked as volunteers in the student cafeteria.

8. *A local convenience store.* The manager of the store sponsored recreational and crafts activities for students on Children's Day, which was held 5 years ago on the school campus. He also has volunteered in classrooms and sat on school committees, including the PTSA, as a community representative.

9. *A nursing home and rehabilitation center.* The center houses 200 patients on five floors. Students provide residents with cards, decorations, and entertainment on holidays, including Christmas, Valentine's Day, and Thanksgiving. Students decorate the main hall of the building as well as residents' rooms. They also visit with the residents and have lunch with them.

10. *A community member.* The community member is an employee at the state's poison center. He regularly volunteers his time at the school to talk to students about poison prevention. He also provides students with educational materials that emphasize the importance of poison proofing their environments. (pp. 1353–1357)

A fourth barrier to implementation involves leadership. Insufficient leadership is commonplace in coordinating and sustaining school-community partnerships. Often the principal cannot do it alone. Successful strategies to overcome this obstacle include "involv[ing] other school groups, like the school leadership council, or PTA" (p. 28). Sanders also reports, "School respondents also suggested building a wide and diverse pool of leaders by providing training on school, family, and community partnerships to the entire school staff, as well as to interested parents and community members" (p. 28).

Another obstacle is inadequate funding to support community alliances. Solutions might include grant-writing initiatives, soliciting donations from local businesses, and holding fund-raisers.

A sixth barrier to implementation of community alliances involves "communication." Lack of or inadequate communication can present an obstacle to any initiative. As principal, you can do much to improve communication. Communication also becomes a barrier when a school is situated in a diverse community in which a high percentage of parents speak a language other than English. Situations such as these can be remedied by hiring translators, disseminating flyers in native languages, as appropriate and feasible, and using a variety of communication networks including e-mail, newsletters, radio, and volunteers to visit homes.

Lack of focus is a final problem that needs your attention. Sometimes the school-community program itself lacks focus or purpose. Careful planning is necessary as is linking community activities to school goals and mission.

Reflective Questions

1. How have you overcome the aforementioned barriers?

2. What other barriers have you encountered and how have you addressed them?

8. BECOME MEDIA SAVVY

Many principals are reluctant to get involved in dealing with the media due to lack of experience and fear that their reports might get misinterpreted or distorted. Community alliances, though, can be strengthened through intelligent use of the media. Savvy principals do not fear the media but rather utilize them as an invaluable resource for communication and public relations, and also to build and sustain good community alliances.

Contacts with the media might be dictated by district policy, so it is wise to consult your district office for guidelines. The following guidelines are culled, in part, from Ubben et al. (2004):

- Establish a plan in advance for dealing with the media (e.g., reporters).
- Consult district office personnel who might have experience with the media.
- Don't provide information that might be misinterpreted.
- Provide the media with prepared statements and relevant photographs if appropriate and prepared well in advance.
- Be aware that media will not cover an event that has already occurred.
- Know media deadlines.
- Realize that the media will, in the end, decide what to report.
- Avoid provoking reporters with "no comment" statements. Rather, help reporters write accurate stories by giving them complete information and background.
- Don't expect that the reporter will know much about how schools operate.
- Avoid jargon in written documents.
- Invite media personnel to the school for special events.
- Prepare press releases.

Reflective Questions

1. Have you had an experience with any form of the media that has been positive or negative? Describe.

2. In what other ways have you dealt with the media?

9. BECOME PART OF A PROFESSIONAL DEVELOPMENT SCHOOL (PDS) INITIATIVE

Establishing a professional relationship with a local college or university is not usually accomplished. Too often principals are unaware of the possibilities, too busy with other matters, or are not encouraged by district office officials to collaborate with colleges. Colleges and universities too are apt to isolate themselves from the lived realities of public school teachers and administrators. Professional development schools (PDSs) are unique ways schools and colleges may collaborate in meaningful ways.

PDS relationships involve deep commitments to bridge the gap between college and school in an effort to promote better student achievement. Echoing this commitment, Levine (2002) states, "Professional development schools bridge the gap between university and school—between theory and practice—to promote student and teacher learning" (p. 65). Schools and colleges share in the responsibility of training future teachers and preparing school children to succeed academically and otherwise. The National Council for the Accreditation of Teacher Education (NCATE) has assumed leadership in promoting and assessing the quality of such partnerships (see http://ncate.org/public/pds Welcome.asp). Parenthetically, you are advised to go to this Web site for much detailed information on the PDS model. The literature is replete with information that highlights the advantages of PDS partnerships to both schools and colleges (see, e.g., Darling-Hammond, 1994; Haskell McBee & Moss, 2002; Levine, 2002; Lyons, 1995; Teitel, 2003).

Many forms of a PDS model are possible. The PDS model offers schools and colleges to partner to create relationships that make sense for that particular situation based on the needs of both sites. As school-community leaders always looking for opportunities to connect with others, you remain cognizant of the PDS opportunity. Principals as school-community leaders will engage in these activities related to the PDS model:

- Take the initiative to seek PDS opportunities by reaching out to college and university faculty in the school or department of education.

- Call meetings with colleagues from institutions of higher learning.
- Offer on-site classroom space for college classes so that courses might be held at the school during the day.
- Provide opportunities for college students to observe, tutor, and teach in classrooms, as appropriate, during the school day.
- Engage with college partners on a plan to develop a PDS model.
- Encourage college faculty to offer in-school workshops.
- Encourage school teachers to attend professional development sessions at the college.
- Encourage school teachers to mentor teacher education candidates.
- Co-plan professional development opportunities for both teachers and professors.
- Share the research about PDS with parents and other community members.
- Develop a Future Teacher's Club (see next page).
- Hire a PDS consultant.
- Seek opportunities to foster student learning and achievement by encouraging professors and teacher candidates to work with teachers and students, respectively.
- Identify school personnel and college faculty to help in the planning and development of the PDS model.
- Work closely with the college dean or chair to ensure a successful PDS model.
- Solicit advice and assistance from parents and other community members.
- Offer incentives to teachers and professors who engage in the PDS model (e.g., released time).
- Keep the focus of the PDS model on promoting opportunities for student learning.
- Encourage colleges to offer on-site graduate courses or programs for teachers.
- Suggest that senior teachers teach graduate courses at the college or university.
- Offer licensed professors to teach at the school site.
- Solicit advice from colleagues in institutions of higher learning.

- Plan for extended instruction opportunities devoted to thematic instruction in content areas so that teacher education candidates can work with students.
- Visit schools that have already developed a PDS partnership.
- Co-develop an assessment system for the PDS model.
- Revise and update PDS model as appropriate, based on assessment data gathered.
- Commit to the PDS model and join together with higher education faculty to utilize the best of both "worlds" to improve student learning and train highly qualified teacher candidates.

PROFESSIONAL DEVELOPMENT SCHOOL (PDS) AT SILVERLAKE SCHOOL IN ANYWHERE, USA, TAKES OFF

Under the leadership of Principal O'Day of the Silverlake School and Dr. Maria Fuentes, education department professor at Silverlake College, the PDS model at Silverlake High School is really taking off. Dr. Fuentes spends at least one full day at the school providing Silverlake faculty professional development workshops. She also supervises Silverlake College student teachers: Neil Benson, Jamie Carr, Marisa Madison, and Sarah Stevenson. Ongoing meetings with the school's principal, Joanne O'Day, faculty, and parents have yielded exciting new ideas to strengthen the partnership between the school and Silverlake College.

One of the exciting new ideas is starting a Future Teacher's Club at the school. Junior and senior students at Silverlake can opt to take an elective course titled "Introduction to Teaching," taught by a Silverlake faculty member who was trained by the Education Department at Silverlake College. Under the proposal, students who spend two years at Silverlake in the program will be eligible to receive a reduction in education coursework if they attend Silverlake College as an undergraduate student.

Students at the high school will study theories and practices of good teaching, covering lesson planning, differentiated instruction, learning styles, inclusion, technology, and much more. Students will visit the Silverlake College campus regularly and attend classes to meet with faculty and students.

Dr. Fuentes hopes that "the program will receive wide acceptance in the community. This project is exciting and enormously

beneficial to help these students get a jump start on their career."
Students will be interviewed before being accepted into the
program. "We are looking for students," explains Dr. Fuentes,
"who demonstrate some enthusiasm for teaching as a career."

Reflective Questions

1. Have you had an experience with a PDS model? Describe.

2. What might you do to develop or further develop a PDS model?

CONCLUSION

According to Sanders and Harvey (2002), "Principal support for
community involvement [is] a central factor in [a] school's success
in developing meaningful community connections" (p. 1360).
School-community leadership is imperative. Without such leadership, valuable opportunities to further advance student learning
and achievement will be squandered. This chapter has highlighted a number of ways you might invite community participation. Certainly, other ways and strategies can be employed.
Constant vigilance is required to pursue community partnerships.
The principalship is continually challenged with a plethora of exi-
gencies that can easily distract even the best principals from their
school-community mission. Too often principals will advocate
such partnerships, but as time proceeds, their interest either
wanes or becomes less of a priority. Here are some research-based
suggestions for keeping the school-community flame alive:

• Write down your commitment to school-community leadership in the form of a simple mission statement. Post it on a
bulletin board in your office so that you notice it from time to time.

• Make sure school-community involvement is part of your
principal evaluation plan. If you know that your superintendent
will be assessing your success in this area, you are more likely to
pay attention to it.

- Collaborate with a colleague from a neighboring school or district. Partnering with a colleague will provide opportunities for mutual discussions and projects.

- Convince others (e.g., teachers, specialists, and other school professionals) to join you in school-community discussions and collaborations. If you feel you're not alone, you'll more likely pursue such ventures,

> *"It takes a village to raise a child."*
> —Ancient African proverb

especially if you can delegate some of the work to other trusted professionals.

- Continue to read about successful school-community collaborations in other schools and districts across the country. Don't feel that you have to reinvent the wheel. You may decide to adopt a model that exists elsewhere. Doing so might reduce stress levels that are inevitable in such ventures.

CHAPTER FOUR

Using Community Resources and Reforms to Close the Black-White Achievement Gap

"When a quality education is denied to children at birth because of their parents' skin color or income, it is not only bad policy, it is immoral."

—Arthur E. Levine

"Those who desire improvements in classroom learning must realize and acknowledge that school reform cannot easily succeed if it ignores the circumstances of their out-of-school lives."

—Richard Rothstein

"A school administrator is an educational leader who promotes the success of all students by collaborating with families and community members, responding to diverse community interests and needs, and mobilizing community resources."

—Interstate School Leaders
Licensure Consortium (ISLLC) Standard

O ne in eight children never graduates from high school. Two in five never complete a single year of college, and every nine seconds a public high school student drops out of school. We spend more money on prisoners than we do to educate our children. Barriers to learning include increased levels of violence, teen pregnancies, depression, eating disorders, sleeping disorders, and not having a family member who cares. Good teaching is certainly necessary, but it's not enough.

Research has demonstrated that social class differences affect student achievement (Rothstein, 2004). Rothstein explains that "parents of different social classes often have different styles of childrearing, different ways of disciplining their children, different ways of communicating expectations, and even different ways of reading to their children" (p. 2). Although he admits that these social class differences "do not express themselves consistently or in the case of every family" (p. 2), patterns or family tendencies on the average can be noted. He explains further:

> That there would be personality and childrearing differences, on average, between families in different social classes makes sense when you think about it: If upper-middle-class parents have jobs where they are expected to collaborate with fellow employees, create new solutions to problems, or wonder how to improve their contributions, they are more likely to talk to their children in ways that differ from the ways of lower-class parents whose own jobs simply require them to follow instructions without question. Children who are raised by parents who are professional will, on average, have more inquisitive attitudes toward the material presented by their teachers than will children who are raised by working-class parents. As a result, no matter how competent the teacher, the academic achievement of lower-class children will, on average, almost inevitably be less than that of middle-class children. The probability of this reduced achievement increases as the characteristics of lower-social-class families accumulate. (p. 2)

He goes on to explain that these social and economic realities can impact student learning. "Lower-class children, on average, have poorer vision than middle-class children, . . . have poorer oral hygiene, more lead poisoning, more asthma, poorer nutrition, less adequate pediatric care, [and] more exposure to smoke" (p. 3). All these conditions affect learning, as Rothstein documents brilliantly in his groundbreaking book.

Rothstein goes on to highlight other social class characteristics that can affect student achievement. For instance, inadequate housing is an important social factor to consider. For example, lower-class children are more likely to live in transitory housing accommodations that can lead to poorer attendance rates in school. Another factor is wealth. Black students from low-income families do not fare as well as their white counterparts, for instance. Rothstein explains:

> It is easier to understand this pattern when we recognize that children can have similar family incomes but be ranked differently in the social class structure, even in economic terms: black families with low income in any year are likely to have been poor for longer than white families with similar income in that year. White families are likely to own far more assets that support their children's achievement than are black families at the same current income level. (p. 3)

In sum, Rothstein posits, children from lower-class families will likely exhibit lower achievement levels than middle-class children. He argues that much of this academic difference in achievement can be attributed to social class characteristics. Rothstein links cultural characteristics with social factors. Cultural differences, for instance, as reflected in the value of education are rooted in social and economic conditions experienced by students from lower classes. He explains, "Black students may value education less than white students because a discriminatory labor market has not historically rewarded black workers for their education—but values persist independently and outlast the economic circumstances that gave rise to them" (p. 4).

Underscoring Rothstein's emphasis on the social and economic factors that affect achievement is the premise that good teaching, high expectations, rigorous standards, accountability, and inspiration are not enough to close the black-white achievement gap. Although these in-school factors can go a long way to close the gap, by themselves they are inadequate. Teachers cannot go it alone. Despite best efforts, some students will not succeed. They will not succeed, in all likelihood, due to social and economic forces beyond the immediate control of a school. Rothstein cautions his readers:

> Readers should not misinterpret this emphasis as implying that better schools are not important, or that school improvement will not make a contribution to narrowing the achievement gap. Better school practices can probably narrow the gap. School reform, however, is not enough. (p. 9)

If social and economic factors play a considerable role in helping to narrow that gap so that all students can learn to the best of their abilities, a critical question must be raised for you, as the school principal. What role can you play in your school and community to narrow this gap and help ensure that all students achieve their academic potential? Of equal importance is the question, What can you do to influence factors external to your school via school-community relations that might also contribute to narrowing this achievement gap? In other words, school-community relations may play a critical role in influencing social agencies, for instance, to play a significant role in assisting school officials (principal, teachers, and counselors) to help each child learn to the best of their ability. Clearly, principals cannot influence certain factors such as parental income levels or access to adequate living quarters. But, through the use of an effective campaign of school-community relations, a principal can solicit the help of a number of social agencies through partnerships. Principals can also strengthen after-school programs to provide needed assistance. Although educators cannot, by themselves, raise achievement levels of lower-class children, they can do much via school-community program development and services.

What You Should Know About Using Community Resources and Reforms to Close the Black-White Achievement Gap

- **School-Community Clinics**—Richard Rothstein's astute and comprehensive recommendations for school reform are highlighted here.
- **Early Childhood Education Centers**—Rothstein's recommendations continue.
- **After-School Programs**—Although recommended by Rothstein, after-school programs are discussed with reference to the work of Fashola.

The following best practices are based on Rothstein's research and suggestions:

1. SCHOOL-COMMUNITY CLINICS

According to Rothstein (2004), "Without fully adequate health care for lower-class children and their parents, there is little hope of fully closing the achievement gap" (p. 138). Principals therefore can assist, although not completely solve this problem, by doing the following:

- Make connections with local health care facilities to establish a health clinic at the school to serve children from disadvantaged homes. You can familiarize yourself with health services, in general, by consulting these Web sites: http://www.mayoclinic.com/; http://www.narhc.org/; and http://www.1-800-schedule.com/. You might visit a local health clinic, establish rapport with local officials, and reach out to local politicians for assistance. Also, providing family health support is an added way that your school can contribute to the health of students and families attending your school. Rothstein (2004) explains the kind of services that could be included:

Clinics associated with schools in lower-class communities should include obstetric and gynecological services for pregnant and postpartum women, pediatric services for children through their high school years, physicians to serve parents of all school-age children, nurses to support these medical services, dentists and hygienists to see both parents and children semi-annually, optometrists and vision therapists to serve those who require treatment for their sight, social workers to refer families to other services, community health educators, and psychologists or therapists to assist families and children who are experiencing excessive stress and other emotional difficulties. (pp. 138–139)

Some would argue that such programs could be costly. According to Rothstein (2004),

Putting dental and vision clinics in schools serving low-income children would cost only about $400 per pupil. . . . This is a lot less money than is often proposed for school reforms like teacher professional development or class size reduction. Schools might get a bigger test score jump, for less money, from dental and vision clinics than from more expensive instructional reforms. (p. 139)

Reflective Questions

1. What have you recently done to provide social welfare information to parents in your community?

2. How would you find the time to get involved in such work?

3. What rationale would you provide to convince a colleague that such efforts will pay off in terms of promoting student achievement?

---

2. EARLY CHILDHOOD EDUCATION CENTERS

The importance of early childhood education in terms of establishing the necessary prerequisites for future student and, even, adult learning is axiomatic. Rothstein (2004) advocates extending early childhood services. Principals can help educate parents in their community of the importance of early childhood education. Rothstein suggests:

Setting up early childhood education centers and services. Research demonstrates that formal education experiences for low-income children that begin at 6 months of age and continues throughout the preschool years can play a significant role in advanced student achievement in later years of schooling. (specific research cited by Rothstein, 2004)

What can you do as a principal to ensure that these children come prepared to learn? Very little you may posit. After all, you have no control over toddler or Head Start programs at your school or community. Yet, forward-thinking school-community principal leaders will reach out to parents of the community to make them aware of such programs that may exist in the community. Affiliations or collaborations with local churches, civic associations, or health centers will give you access to parents of preschool children. Serve as a guest lecturer where you can review the plethora of early childhood research that demonstrates the impact of toddler and preschool experiences on academic achievement in school. You can explain to them that day care settings do not offer the necessary enrichment their children will need to succeed. Formal early childhood programs are more content rich and are usually staffed with licensed, credentialed teachers. Explain to them what Rothstein (2004) states: "To narrow the achievement gap later in life, lower-class toddlers probably should begin early childhood programs at six months of age, and attend for a full day" (p. 140). Clearly, you can serve as an advocate in your interactions with local politicians to urge them to support such early childhood programs.

Reflective Questions

1. What kinds of workshops can you offer to address this best practice?

2. To which community groups can you speak and what would be the essential message of your speech?

---

3. AFTER-SCHOOL PROGRAMS

Research demonstrates consistently that structured after-school programs contribute to narrowing the achievement gap (Rothstein,

2004). Fashola's (2002) in-depth treatment of after-school programs provides a rationale for their importance, cites examples of effective programs, and offers concrete suggestions for implementation. Fashola highlights the following benefits of such programs in concise fashion:

- Improves academic performance across content areas
- Provides academic enrichment
- Offers social, cultural, and recreational activities

Too often, however, these programs lack academic rigor and become little more than "babysitting" services. Moreover, these after-school programs are usually disconnected from curricula offered during the regular school day. Principals can do much here by solidifying this connection, thus ensuring continuity between day and after-school programs. Moreover, the principal can and should insist that such programs and activities meet the highest academic standards in curriculum and instruction. Principals can offer supervision (Sullivan & Glanz, 2005) to these after-school programs so that highest standards of instruction are maintained. Certainly, some might argue that having already overworked principals oversee after-school programs is as much impractical as it is idealistic. Still, school-community leadership that is aimed at comprehensive reforms in and out of school, even before and after school, are more likely to have a lasting impact on closing the achievement gap and thus ensuring high achievement for all students. As transformative school-community leaders, principals must take an assertive stance by either paying attention to these after-school programs (which can, when done well, support in-school instruction during the day) or working toward creating more effective after-school programs. Fashola (2002) identifies the following steps in creating after-school programs:

- Create and conduct a needs assessment. As principal, you can proactively assess community-school needs by speaking with parents, teachers, students, and other community partners to ascertain the specific academic needs of students who attend after-school programs. For instance, for students who do not possess computers at home, after-school workshops or classes can be offered to teach students PowerPoint, databasing, and word processing. A needs assessment, conducted in various ways, can provide substance and guidance for such programs. Fashola advises educators to involve all parties in designing such programs:

> For example, a program might decide to create a well-rounded, after-school program and set the hours of the program from 2:30 p.m. to 5 p.m., but forget to consult with the parents of the students. This could be a problem because of the hours of operation. Parents may like the program and actually be in need of the services, but the hours of operation could be a hindrance to the participation of the students. Involving parents in the goals by setting sessions that address stakeholders' wants, needs, and concerns would encourage the program to address transportation issues by either extending the hours of the program or by providing some transportation option for the participants. (pp. 58–59)

• Create committees and execute goals. Establishing goals is critical to a program's success. Solicit involvement from interested parties. Fashola explains:

> For example, if one of the goals was to improve the reading skills of students, the academics committee—headed by a staff member with training in the area of reading programs—would be responsible for the curriculum, materials, and training of other staff members. (p. 59)

• Create the components. Many decisions have to be made about the program including, among others, who will attend, who will serve as staff, what funding is required, and how to recruit, train, and retain staff. Fashola identifies three major components that need attention during program implementation: academic, recreational, and cultural. About the academic component, Fashola states, "The school or community center must decide whether the goal of its academic component is to improve the school-day performance of children through activities tied to the school curriculum, through enrichment activities, or through both" (p. 60). He goes on to say that careful attention to hiring qualified educators to teach in the program should be a top priority. Research that Fashola reviews indicates that successful after-school academic programs have "clear goals, well-developed procedures for attaining those goals, and extensive professional development" (p. 61).

Establishing meaningful and content-rich after-school programs can go far toward making an academic difference. Proactive principals pay attention to as many factors that affect student achievement as possible. The school-community leader realizes the important value of such an effort.

Reflective Question

1. What are your reactions to Rothstein's suggestions and to your role as principal in helping facilitate these reforms?

CONCLUSION

As a society, we have not been willing to commit to fundamental change to provide the highest-quality education to all students regardless of socioeconomic background. Educational reform, although important, is inadequate, by itself, to meet the needs of all students. Jean Anyon (1997), scholar and educator, reminds us that school reform without social and economic reform is like washing air on one side of a screen door—it makes no sense and accomplishes nothing. Moreover, Larry Cuban (1993), noted educational historian, demonstrates and reminds us that top-down driven change has not had a remarkable history. Reform efforts are likely to fail when reforms do not address the underlying bureaucratic structure of schooling, and the social and economic structures that support schools. Current proposals, couched to some degree by increased parental and community involvement and elimination of some bureaucratic and inefficient layers of bureaucracy, do not go far enough to dismantle a dysfunctional system of schooling.

"In a sense, moving from an ordinary school to a community of hope is a kind of psychological magic. But we can make this magic happen by . . . providing the context for both the school and the individual members of the school community to realize their potential."

—Thomas J. Sergiovanni

So what can you, as a principal, do? Principals should serve as transformative school-community leaders. Young (2004) affirms such a role for the principal.

> Principals must be accountable to their communities and make citizens aware of the inadequacies and unfairness of a system that continually privileges the rich over the poor. . . . Principals have the social power and influence to make a difference. . . . [Principals should] speak up and make people aware of the realities we know so well. (p. 109)

Principals of the 21st century are no longer merely maintainers and sustainers of the status quo. As school-community leader, your moral commitment to ensuring the highest educational opportunities for all students is more critical than ever. You remain committed to doing everything and anything in your power to support high achievement for all students. You rally educational and social support, even political, to raise the consciousness of the school community and the community at large to engage in comprehensive reform. As school-community leader, you are a staunch spokesperson for justice, equity, and opportunity for all.

Conclusion

Making School-Community Relations a Reality

This book has underscored the too-often taken-for-granted role of principals as school-community leaders. We reviewed best practices of reaching out to parents and working to solidify a range of community alliances. Each of these best practices helps support, in direct and indirect ways, student learning and, ultimately, achievement. In Chapter 4, the case was made to expand the influence of the principal in terms of contributing to more holistic reform efforts by serving, at the least, as an advocate for social and economic reforms. You realize as principal that educational reforms alone are inadequate to compensate for social and economic inequities that exist in the community. As principal, you should not abrogate your responsibility to address holistic reform. Transformational leadership, indeed, becomes a moral imperative of today's principal leader. Principals actualize such leadership in work that involves relationships between school and community.

> *"When properly executed, community involvement in schools can be the little extra that makes the big difference."*
>
> —Joyce L. Epstein et al.

Some final suggestions for making school-community leadership a reality include, among others, the following:

- Examine and clarify your beliefs about your school-community role and ability (efficacy) to make a difference as principal.

- Learn from principals who you know to be school-community leader exemplars.
- Become conversant with the literature and research on school-community relations and leadership.
- Demonstrate your commitment to school-community relations in word and deed.
- Invite a range of community members to participate in meaningful activities, even decisions, about the school.
- Solicit assistance and support from central office personnel and from the superintendent, in particular.
- Take risks to involve others, and seek support from teachers and other school personnel.
- Assess your role as school-community leader; involve others in the assessment process.
- Reach out to specific agencies for assistance by proposing specific projects and ways they can assist your school.
- Don't be shy or reticent; remain assertive, albeit not pushy.
- Offer community partners a built-in incentive for them to participate.
- Devote time and energy to forging and sustaining relationships in the community.

Resource A

Realities of School-Community Leadership: In-Basket Simulations

This section highlights some of the realities of school-community leadership using an approach called "In-Basket Simulations." It is a study technique derived from an approach used when I studied for licensure as a principal in New York City. The approach was developed by the Institute for Research and Professional Development (http://www.nycenet .edu/opm/opm/profservices/rfp1b723.html). Scenarios that you as a principal might encounter are presented for your reaction. For instance, "A letter from an irate parent complaining that her child is intentionally being ignored during instruction in class by the teacher is sent to your attention. What would you do?" Challenging you to confront real-life phenomena under controlled conditions, these simulated in-basket items will prompt critical inquiry.

Here are suggestions to guide you as you complete these in-basket exercises:

1. Think and respond as if you are a principal, not a teacher or, perhaps, an assistant principal.

2. Place yourself mentally in each situation as if the case was actually happening to you.

3. Draw on your experiences and from what you've learned from others. Think of a principal you respect and ask yourself, "What would Principal X have done?"

4. Make distinctions between actions you would personally take and actions you would delegate to others.

5. Utilize resources (personnel or otherwise) to assist you.

6. Think about your response; then share it with a colleague for her or his reaction.

7. Record your response. A day later, re-read the scenario and your response. Would you still have reacted the same way?

During an interview you are asked to respond to the following scenarios:

• You are a newly appointed principal to an intermediate school in which the former principal never considered community interests nor solicited community members' involvement in any way. You want to encourage school-community relations. What are the first steps you'd take?

• Your superintendent informs you that several parents have registered formal complaints that their views and opinions are ignored at your school. You're asked to explain your parental involvement program as well as to react to these complaints.

• You are a high school principal in which several for-profit companies want to set up advertisement bulletin boards, of varying sizes, in your school. Would you allow such ads, if it would increase budget revenues for the school by $40,000 per year?

• A local politician wishes to donate $20,000 in new technologies for your school. Would you accept the offer?

• Two parent groups vie for power in your urban middle school. Elections are weeks away. Each group approaches you for its support. What stance would you take?

• A wealthy alumnus contacts you that she wants to donate $500,000 to the school, but stipulates that she wants the money geared for the music education program in your school. You already have a thriving and well-equipped music department and facilities at your suburban high school. You need the money, however, to increase funds for a new literacy-based program that could assist your efforts to increase literacy scores on standardized achievement tests. How would you go about approaching this donor to allow you to use the money with more flexibility? How would you react if she refused, insisting on overseeing how the money will be spent?

• You are a principal of a high school that has experienced enormous demographic changes. The majority of students now come from families considered below the poverty line. Demographic changes include lower achievement levels on standardized test scores across the curriculum, lack of parental involvement in the school, and a diminishment of business partnerships with the school. What concrete steps would you take to increase parental involvement and solicit businesses to reinvest in the schools? How would encouraging greater parental involvement and business participation affect student achievement in your school?

• Mr. Smith, principal of Bishops High School in an urban area of a medium-sized city, realizes how important it is to look good to the community. He continually bombards the media (i.e., newspapers, radio, etc.) with ads and information about the school's athletic program. The school's basketball team won the State championship twice in the last 3 years. Most, if not all of the school's ads in the community center around athletics. The superintendent calls Mr. Smith into a meeting and congratulates him on such winning efforts and applauds his media savvy. However, he gently suggests to the principal that his future ads should focus on non-athletic school events, and especially, on academic student accomplishments. How would you use the media to bring positive public relations (PR) to your school? Describe your PR campaign in detail, why it's important, and what potential impact it may have on student achievement, if any.

• You are a principal in a midwestern, urban high school in which parents of Mexican descent complain that there is a lack of attention to their cultural traditions as reflected in the school curriculum. The school's population of students of Mexican descent is the third largest, comprising 21% of the student body. How would you approach this situation?

- As principal of a middle school, you have several creative ways to increase parental involvement and attract local business to donate funds to support the new computer lab in the school. Unfortunately, you find little support from your superintendent. In fact, she insists that you, as principal, should be more involved in in-school matters and that you should leave community networking to her. Generally, you and the superintendent do not see eye-to-eye on many matters. In the past, words have been exchanged between the two of you, and no love is lost on most matters. You understand the value of strong community involvement by the principal. How would you work with the superintendent to support your continued efforts in school-community relations?

- Parents complain about a teacher, Mr. Carson, who displays an uninviting demeanor when meeting with parents. One parent complained, "Mr. Carson places all the chairs up on the desk in his room, as if the room is being mopped by the custodian. He speaks to parents while standing up. Consequently, discussions are usually very brief. This is an outrage." How would you confront Mr. Carson about such complaints?

- You find yourself too busy to interact much with the external community. Your primary emphasis during the first three years as principal of an urban elementary school has been to raise reading scores as reflected on standardized tests. After being charged by the superintendent "to get out there," how would you solicit community involvement to directly and indirectly participate to improve student achievement in reading?

- Teachers complain that because children "have so many home problems and parents are not involved," they (the teachers) cannot "help" them. What's your reaction? What actions would you take?

- Parents complain that the after-school program is "just a babysitting service." They demand that you increase the program's academic rigor. How would you react to such complaints?

- Local corporation X turns down your request for a $60,000 grant to support computer technology in your school. What's your next step?

- You've heard from a colleague that some grant money from a state senator's office is available to support your efforts at establishing an after-school tutorial program. What steps would you take to secure the $450,000 grant? Whose assistance would you solicit?

- Parents inform you that they want a more active voice in curricular decision making in your school. Furthermore, they insist on being consulted on all new teacher hires. How would you respond to such demands?

- The superintendent receives complaints from teachers of your suburban elementary school that you pay too much attention to community interests. They say you're more interested in parents' concerns than listening to them. The word about school is that "the principal is a politician, not an educator." One lead teacher in your school complained that you are "a showman, only after the glitz. . . . There's no academic substance to his efforts." He continues, "Sure, the principal brings in these famous actors, politicians, and others, but all he does is showcase our work to them. His only interest is to make himself look good." Admittedly, you do pay an inordinate amount of attention to the community. Yet, you feel that, in the long run, such community outreach can only benefit the school. How would you go about communicating these benefits to teachers and others? How precisely do these efforts affect student achievement?

- During a speech you inadvertently offend some parents for their lack of attendance at school meetings. Your comments spread like wildfire throughout the community. How would you handle this irate call?

Parent: I heard what you said. I do care for my child. I just had to work late that night. How dare you imply that I do not care!

- What role would you play in terms of addressing social, political, and/or economic reform in order to promote learning for all students in your school?

Resource B

*Assessing Your Role in
School-Community Relations*

As the principal, you realize that your responsibility and influence does not stop at the front door of the school building. By bridging school with community, you are better able to connect with individuals and groups in order to support your school mission that includes, above all else, to promote student learning. Please complete this questionnaire as a means of self-reflection or analysis in order to assess the extent to which you share a school-community vision. This survey instrument might also give you some ideas of interacting with the community that you have not thought about. You realize, of course, that the survey is not scientific, and results therefore should be studied in that light. Please note that your responses are private. Your honest responses to the various items below will best serve as reflective tools to assist you in becoming an even better school-community leader.

SA = Strongly Agree ("For the most part, yes.")

 A = Agree ("Yes, but . . .")

 D = Disagree ("No, but . . .")

SD = Strongly Disagree ("For the most part, no.")

SA   A   D   SD   1. I undertake a yearly poll to ascertain parental views on school matters.

SA   A   D   SD   2. I am willing to listen to advice from parents and community members.

SA A D SD   3. I speak to community groups once a month, on average.

SA A D SD   4. I encourage parents to join curriculum committees.

SA A D SD   5. I am politically active in the community by speaking, on occasion, to local politicians and other community members.

SA A D SD   6. I have a school-community relations program firmly established, implemented, and reviewed annually.

SA A D SD   7. I am aware of the average income levels of parents in my school community.

SA A D SD   8. I am fully aware of the ethnic and racial compositions of parents in my community as well as their cultural traditions.

SA A D SD   9. I am in contact with key elected officials in my community.

SA A D SD   10. I know the opinion makers in my community.

SA A D SD   11. I am quite familiar with the geography of the community in which my school is situated.

SA A D SD   12. Within the district in which I work, I visit some sort of community function (outside my school) at least once a month.

SA A D SD   13. I am acutely aware of community health and safety problems and issues within the district in which I work.

SA   A   D   SD   14. I am aware of community recreational
                          and youth programs in my community.

SA   A   D   SD   15. I serve as a member on at least one
                          type of civic organization.

SA   A   D   SD   16. I see my role as fostering
                          communication between my
                          school and the community.

SA   A   D   SD   17. I discuss the importance of school-
                          community relations, along with
                          relaying specific information, to my
                          faculty and staff.

SA   A   D   SD   18. Teachers can assist school-community
                          relations by their own voluntary
                          contacts with the community.

SA   A   D   SD   19. I sometimes invite faculty and staff to
                          partake in community activities.

SA   A   D   SD   20. I invite community representatives to
                          visit my school as often as is relevant
                          and possible.

SA   A   D   SD   21. I am aware of the various alternative
                          educational resources that exist in the
                          community beyond what is offered at
                          my school.

SA   A   D   SD   22. I encourage family and community
                          involvement in decision making.

SA   A   D   SD   23. I believe in professional development
                          schools (PDSs) as a unique opportunity
                          to foster school-community
                          involvement.

SA A D SD   24. My building is usually available for use by community organizations, when approved by district officials and in accordance with local regulations and laws.

SA A D SD   25. My P.T.A. is actively engaged in the community as well as with a variety of in-school functions.

SA A D SD   26. I encourage teachers to take students on field trips to local cultural centers, such as museums and libraries.

SA A D SD   27. I have developed a school-community strategic plan.

SA A D SD   28. Our school has developed a written plan of policies and administrative support for family involvement.

SA A D SD   29. I solicit free educational resources from local businesses and organizations.

SA A D SD   30. I reach out to service clubs that may include Lions, Rotary, Knights of Columbus, and so forth.

SA A D SD   31. I encourage family and community involvement in homework.

SA A D SD   32. I partake in at least one social, civic, or religious association in my own community.

SA A D SD   33. I encourage class reunions, community cultural gatherings, and other varied community-school functions.

SA   A   D   SD   34. I solicit assistance from senior
                         citizens in the community.

SA   A   D   SD   35. I keep faculty and staff aware of
                         community resources, events, and
                         activities.

SA   A   D   SD   36. I solicit business or social agency
                         volunteers to work in my school, as
                         appropriate.

SA   A   D   SD   37. I reach out to religious institutions
                         in my community to find ways of
                         soliciting their assistance with school
                         objectives.

SA   A   D   SD   38. I reach out to the local employers in the
                         school community, including the local
                         grocery stores.

SA   A   D   SD   39. I call on charities such as the American
                         Red Cross and the United Way.

SA   A   D   SD   40. I encourage family and community
                         involvement in fund-raising.

SA   A   D   SD   41. I contact alumni who play a critical role
                         in school-community relations.

SA   A   D   SD   42. I reach out to local colleges to support
                         the professional development of my
                         teachers and others.

SA   A   D   SD   43. I have contacted local hospitals and
                         other health-related agencies to share
                         information.

SA   A   D   SD   44. I keep the community informed in
                         various ways (letters, bulletins,
                         calendars, posters, newspaper ads, etc.)
                         of significant school events (e.g., talent
                         shows, honor ceremonies).

SA   A   D   SD   45. My school has PR (public relations) brochures and materials ready for distribution to the community.

SA   A   D   SD   46. I contact the local radio station to make relevant announcements.

SA   A   D   SD   47. I have invited media to my school to cover a special event or activity.

SA   A   D   SD   48. I know the names and have the phone numbers of key community officials, including the police department, hospital or emergency medical team, radio, newspaper, church, and so on.

SA   A   D   SD   49. I articulate on a regular basis with other elementary, middle, or high schools.

SA   A   D   SD   50. Our school newsletter highlights, in most issues, some aspect of the community (e.g., a civic official).

SA   A   D   SD   51. I undertake fund-raising initiatives in the local community and encourage others to do so, as appropriate.

SA   A   D   SD   52. I continually invite local community officials, including employers and politicians, to my school to discuss ways of furthering partnerships.

SA   A   D   SD   53. I maintain contact with the editor of the local newspaper to advertise school-community events and to solicit assistance for the school in relevant ways.

SA   A   D   SD   54. I discuss with my faculty ways to improve parental involvement and other community involvement in schools.

SA   A   D   SD   55. I undertake an annual evaluation of our school-community relations program.

SA   A   D   SD   56. I solicit feedback from parents, informally and formally, about school-community relations.

SA   A   D   SD   57. My role is to maximize community resources in order to promote student learning in my school.

SA   A   D   SD   58. I am committed to school-community relations and will develop sufficient time to ensure my school's success.

SA   A   D   SD   59. I cannot succeed at school-community relations without the assistance of my teachers.

SA   A   D   SD   60. The most obvious way to ensure a sound school-community relations program is to develop organizational mechanisms that facilitate smooth, ongoing, and productive communications between parents and teachers. Parents must play an active role in school, whenever feasible.

Analyze your responses:
Although the items above do not fit easily into only one category, examine the groupings below to assess your role as school-community leader:

Items that demonstrate your commitment to school-community leadership and relations:
16, 17, 23, 26, 30, 35, 45, 49, 51, 53, 55, 57, 58

Items that demonstrate the extent of your awareness of community:
7, 8, 10, 11, 13, 14, 21, 44, 48, 50

Items that indicate you have established a school-community plan:
6, 27, 28

Items that indicate your involvement with community on an ongoing basis:
3, 5, 9, 12, 15, 20, 24, 29, 32, 33, 34, 37, 38, 39, 42, 43, 47, 52

Items that indicate the roles of teachers in school-community involvement:
18, 19, 54, 59

Items that indicate the roles of parents in school-community involvement:
25, 31, 56, 60

Items that indicate your willingness to invite parents and community members to join important curriculum committees and contribute to other relevant school work:
1, 2, 4, 22, 36, 40, 41

Items that demonstrate your commitment to school-community relations:
16, 17, 26, 30, 35, 51, 57, 58

Resource C

An Annotated Bibliography
of Best Resources

The literature on the principalship and related areas is extensive. The list below is not meant to serve as a comprehensive resource by any means. The selected titles I have annotated are few but, in my opinion, are among the most useful references on the subject. Rather than "impress" you with a more extensive list, I have selected these outstanding works related to school-community leadership that will supplement my book quite well. I may have missed, of course, other important works. Nevertheless, this list is a good start. Don't forget that life is a long journey of continuous learning. Continue to hone your skills by reading good books and journal articles on school-community leadership. No one is ever perfect and everyone can learn something new by keeping current with the literature in the field. Share your readings and reactions with a colleague.

Community Involvement

Decker, L. E., & Decker, V. A. (2003). *Home, school, and community partnerships.* Lanham, MD: Scarecrow Press.

> Easy-to-read guide with practical and proven strategies for creating and sustaining home-school-community partnerships.

Dodd, A. W., & Konzal, J. K. (2002). *How communities build stronger schools: Stories, strategies and promising practices for educating every child.* New York: Palgrave Macmillan.

> Practical tips and testimonials for encouraging meaningful community involvement. Presents a comprehensive look at community involvement in a readable way.

Epstein, J. L., Sanders, M. G., Simon, B. S., Salinas, K. C., Jansorn, N. R., & Van Voorhis, F. L. (2002). *School, family, and community partnerships: Your handbook for action* (2nd ed.). Thousand Oaks, CA: Corwin.

As the title implies, this handbook, written by a foremost authority in the field, is packed with tools and strategies that help build meaningful school partnerships. Specific programs and practices are highlighted with steps for implementation. This is an invaluable resource guide to help generate creative ideas and concrete proposals to build and sustain community partnerships.

Fashola, O. S. (2002). *Building effective afterschool programs.* Thousand Oaks, CA: Corwin.

One of the best books on the topic, this book discusses the importance of whole community involvement to provide the highest level of education possible after school. Principal involvement in after-school programs contributes to improving academic achievement for all students.

Kindred, L., Bagain, D., & Gallagher, D. (1997). *The school and community relations* (6th ed.). Boston: Allyn & Bacon.

One of the better textbooks on the topic, this book highlights theory but also offers concrete proposals and suggestions.

McEwan, E. K. (2005). *How to deal with parents who are angry, troubled, afraid, or just plain crazy* (2nd ed.). Thousand Oaks, CA: Corwin.

An excellent, highly readable, enjoyable, and practical book every principal should read. Will help you avert potential problems and brainstorm solutions for seemingly intractable solutions.

Video Resource on Community Involvement

Institute for Responsive Education (Producer). (2003). *Principals speak out* [videotape]. (Available from http://www.responsiveeducation.org/publications.html)

This 25-minute video interviews three principals with highly successful parent and community connections and programs in their schools. Offers sound rationales for community partnerships, reviews community-school relations benefits, and highlights advice on how to foster meaningful community-school partnerships.

Web Resources on Community Involvement

Center on School, Family and Community Partnerships, http://www.csos.jhu.edu/p2000/center.htm

The Center at Johns Hopkins University, run by noted director Joyce Epstein, contains a wealth of inexpensive resources, print and nonprint, on building and sustaining community partnerships.

National Center for Family and Community Connections with Schools at
the Southwest Educational Development Laboratory, http://www
.sedl.org/connections/

National Community Education Association, http://www.ncea.com

National Network of Partnership Schools at Johns Hopkins University,
http://www.csos.jhu.edu/p2000/ and http://www.partnership
schools.org

Provides professional development training for school, family, and
community partnerships.

Parental Involvement

Lawrence-Lightfoot, S. (2003). *The essential conversation: What parents
and teachers can learn from each other.* New York: Random House.

According to one reviewer, this is an "eloquent, passionately moving
and illuminating book." An in-depth analysis of the parent-teacher
relationship. Insightful, practical, and a must-read.

Video Resource on Parent Involvement

Association for Supervision and Curriculum Development (Producer).
(1998). *How to create successful parent-student conferences* [videotape].
(Available from http://shop.ascd.org/productdisplay.cfm?productid
=498041)

This 15-minute videotape is part of the Association for Supervision
and Curriculum Development's "How to" video series. Actual
teachers demonstrate ways to create better partnerships with
parents. Topics include the first step to take when planning every conference, how to deal with an irate parent, examples of "door-opening
statements" that encourage conversation, how to use portfolios of
student work in conferences, and what to do after a conference.

Web Resources on Parental Involvement

Center for Education Reform, http://www.edreform.com/index.cfm?fuse
Action=section&pSectionID=5&CFID=45187&CFTOKEN=40897536

National Association of Elementary School Principals, http://www
.naesp.org

National Association of Secondary School Principals, http://www
.nassp.org

National Coalition for Parent Involvement in Education (NCPIE), http://
www.ncpie.org/AboutNCPIE/

An outstanding Web site that serves as an advocate for the involvement of parents and families in schools; fosters relationships between

home, school, and community to enhance the educational experience of students. Packed with information and strategies.

Project Parents, Inc., http://www.projectparents.org/job.php
Project for School Innovation, http://www.psinnovation.org

Public Relations

Bagin, D., Ferguson, D., & Marx, G. (1985). *Public relations for administrators.* Arlington, VA: American Association of School Administrators.

Work in public relations is necessarily part of the responsibilities of a school-community leader. Although touched on to some extent in *What Every Principal Should Know About School-Community Leadership,* you should familiarize yourself with the topic; thus, Bagin et al.'s book is very useful.

Cutlip, S. M., Center, A. H., & Broom, G. M. (1994). *Effective public relations* (7th ed.). Englewood Cliffs, NJ: Prentice Hall.

A highly readable text on the topic.

Best Book on Community, Parent, and Public Relations

Fiore, D. J. (2002). *School community relations.* Larchmont, NY: Eye on Education.

Identifying school-community relations as essential to school leadership, this comprehensive book examines the topic in depth from a variety of perspectives. Well-researched and documented, this volume is a must-read for the principal wanting to strengthen relations with the community. Among the topics not usually included in similar books are multiculturalism, organizational standards, overcoming communication barriers, intergenerational programs in schools, improving media relations, and crisis management plans.

References

Anyon, J. (1997). *Ghetto schooling: A political economy of urban educational reform.* New York: Teachers College Press.

Arriaza, G. (2004). Making changes that stay made: School reform and community involvement. *The High School Journal, 87*(4), 10–24.

Buchen, I. H. (2003). Education in America: The next 25 years. *The Futurist, 37*(1), 44–50.

Chavkin, N. F. (2000). Family and community involvement policies: Teachers can lead the way. *The Clearing House, 73*(5), 287–293.

Cotton, K. (2003). *Principals and student achievement: What research says.* Alexandria, VA: Association for Supervision and Curriculum Development.

Cuban, L. (1993). *How teachers taught: Constancy and change in American classrooms, 1890–1990* (2nd ed.). New York: Teachers College Press.

Darling-Hammond, L. (1994). *Professional development schools: Schools for developing a profession.* New York: Teachers College Press.

Davis, S. H. (1998). Taking aim at effective leadership. *Thrust for Educational Leadership, 28*(2), 6–9.

Elmore, R. (1999). *Leadership of large-scale improvement in American education.* Washington, DC: Albert Shanker Institute.

Epstein, J. L., & Salinas, K. C. (2004). Partnering with families and communities. *Educational Leadership, 62*(3), 12–18.

Epstein, J. L., Sanders, M. G., Simon, B. S., Salinas, K. C., Jansorn, N. R., & Van Voorhis, F. L. (2002). *School, family, and community partnerships: Your handbook for action* (2nd ed.). Thousand Oaks, CA: Corwin.

Fashola, O. S. (2002). *Building effective afterschool programs.* Thousand Oaks, CA: Corwin.

Fiore, D. J. (2002). *School-community relations.* Larchmont, NY: Eye on Education.

Fullan, M. (1999). *Change forces: The sequel.* London: Falmer Press.

Glanz, J., & Sullivan, S. (2000). *Supervision in practice: Three steps to improving teaching and learning.* Thousand Oaks, CA: Corwin.

Goldberg, M. (2001). *Lessons from exceptional school leaders.* Alexandria, VA: Association for Supervision and Curriculum Development.

Gretz, P. (2003). School and community partnerships: Cultivating friends. *Principal Leadership, 3*(5), 32–35.

Haskell McBee, R., & Moss, J. (2002). PDS partnerships come of age. *Educational Leadership, 59*(4), 61–64.

Haynes, N. M., & Emmons, C. L. (1997). *Comer school development program effects: A ten year review, 1986–1996.* New Haven, CT: Yale University Child Study Center.

Henderson, A. T., & Berla, N. (1994). *A new generation of evidence: The family is critical to student achievement.* Washington, DC: Center for Law and Education.

Henderson, A. T., & Mapp, K. L. (2002). *A new wave of evidence: The impact of school, family and community connections on student achievement.* Austin, TX: Southwest Educational Development Laboratory.

Lawrence-Lightfoot, S. (2003). *The essential conversation: What parents and teachers can learn from each other.* New York: Random House.

Leithwood, K., Seashore Louis, K., Anderson, S., & Wahlstrom, K. (2004). *How leadership influences student learning.* Minneapolis: Center for Applied Research and Educational Improvement, University of Minnesota.

Levine, A. E. (2004). Preface. In R. Rothstein, *Class and schools: Using social, economic, and educational reform to close the black-white achievement gap* (pp. x–xi). New York: Teachers College Press.

Levine, M. (2002). Why invest in professional development schools? *Educational Leadership, 59*(4), 65–67.

Lyons, N. (1995). Creating a professional development school: From conversation to relationships, resolve, and sustainability. *Quality Teaching, 4*(2), 4–6.

Mamchak, P. S., & Mamchak, S. R. (1983). *School administrator's public speaking portfolio.* San Francisco: Jossey-Bass.

Marzano, R. J. (2003). *What works in schools: Translating research into action.* Alexandria, VA: Association for Supervision and Curriculum Development.

Marzano, R. J., Pickering, D. J., & Pollock, J. E. (2001). *Classroom instruction that works: Research-based strategies for increasing student achievement.* Alexandria, VA: Association for Supervision and Curriculum Development.

Reynolds, M. (2002). Bringing your school closer to your community. *Principal Leadership (Middle Level Ed.), 3*(2), 81–82.

Rothstein, R. (2004). *Class and schools: Using social, economic, and educational reform to close the black-white achievement gap.* New York: Teachers College Press.

Sadker, D., & Sadker, M. (2000). *Teachers, schools, and society.* New York: McGraw-Hill.

Sanders, M. G. (2001). The role of "community" in comprehensive school, family and community partnership programs. *The Elementary School Journal, 102*(1), 19–34.

Sanders, M. G., & Harvey, A. (2002). Beyond the school walls: A case study of principal leadership for school-community collaboration. *Teachers College Record, 104*(7), 1345–1368.

Sergiovanni, T. J. (1995). *Leadership for the schoolhouse.* San Francisco: Jossey-Bass.

Starratt, R. J., & Howells, M. L. (1998). Supervision as moral agency. In G. R. Firth & E. F. Pajak (Eds.), *Handbook of research on school supervision* (pp. 987–1005). New York: Macmillan.

Sullivan, S., & Glanz, J. (2005). *Supervision that improves teaching: Strategies and techniques* (2nd ed.). Thousand Oaks, CA: Corwin.

Teitel, L. (2003). *Professional development schools: Starting, sustaining, and assessing partnerships that improve student learning.* Thousand Oaks, CA: Corwin.

Thompson, M. (2005, February 21). Parent-teacher conferences: Eight steps to parental success. *Time,* p. 49.

Trotter, A., Honawar, V., & Tonn, J. L. (2005, January 12). U.S. schools find lessons in tsunami. *Education Week, 24*(18), 1, 2.

Ubben, G. C., Hughes, L. W., & Norris, C. J. (2004). *The principal: Creative leadership for excellence in schools* (5th ed.). Boston: Allyn & Bacon.

Whitaker, T., & Fiore, D. J. (2001). *Dealing with difficult parents: And with parents in difficult situations.* Larchmont, NY: Eye on Education.

Wilmore, E. L. (2002). *Principal leadership: Applying the new Educational Leadership Constituent Council (ELCC) standards.* Thousand Oaks, CA: Corwin.

Young, P. G. (2004). *You have to go to school—You're the principal: 101 tips to make it better for your students, your staff, and yourself.* Thousand Oaks, CA: Corwin.

Index

Note: Page references marked (*f*) are figures.

**CORWIN
PRESS**

The Corwin Press logo—a raven striding across an open book—represents the union of courage and learning. Corwin Press is committed to improving education for all learners by publishing books and other professional development resources for those serving the field of PreK–12 education. By providing practical, hands-on materials, Corwin Press continues to carry out the promise of its motto: **"Helping Educators Do Their Work Better."**